THE BOOK OF
Light Italian
DISHES

THE BOOK OF
Light Italian
DISHES

MAXINE CLARK

Photographed by
SIMON BUTCHER

PUBLISHED BY
SALAMANDER BOOKS LIMITED
LONDON

Published by Salamander Books Limited
8 Blenheim Court, Brewery Road, London N7 9NT

ISBN 1 84065 272 1

A member of the Chrysalis Group plc

Managing Editor: Anne McDowall
Editor: Felicity Jackson
Designer: Paul Johnson
Photographer: Simon Butcher
Photographer's Assistant: Giles Stokoe
Home Economist: Nicola Fowler
Home Economist's Assistant: Becky Johnson
Stylist: Vicky Zentner
Colour separation: PixelTech Pte, Singapore
Filmset: SX DTP
Printed in Spain

Acknowledgment:
The publishers would like to thank Meyer (UK) Ltd.
for supplying saucepans.

Notes:
All spoon measurements are level.
1 teaspoon = 5 ml spoon
1 tablespoon = 15 ml spoon

CONTENTS

INTRODUCTION

Italian cooking brings all the flavours and sunshine of the Mediterranean into your kitchen, and with *The Book of Light Italian Dishes* you can bring all the additional benefits of the Mediterranean diet to your lifestyle. Using olive oil to replace animal fat, and incorporating small amounts of meat and pasta with maximum amounts of fish and vegetables, Italian food can be lightened to suit our hectic modern way of life.

A feast of over 80 recipes, from healthy hearty soups, easy starters, pastas, pizzas and risottos, delicious fish, light poultry and meat dishes, a variety of vegetable accompaniments, to luscious low-fat desserts. Each recipe is illustrated in full colour, with clear step-by-step instructions, to make light Italian cooking as quick and easy as possible.

LIGHT ITALIAN COOKING

Italian food can be lightened to suit our modern low-fat, high fibre diet without losing the taste and depth of flavour. The use of good quality fresh ingredients is essential for the best flavour and texture. Use ingredients seasonally, when they are freshest and the flavour is most intense.

BREADS, PULSES AND BEANS
Each region of Italy has its own speciality bread from the saltless, and rather tasteless, Tuscan bread to the "ciabatta" or slipper bread made with olive oil, and focaccia in all its shapes and sizes.

Bread is an essential part of any meal in Italy, being both nutritious and filling, and providing essential roughage. It is often toasted over charcoal, rubbed with garlic and drizzled with a little olive oil and served as a starter – the original "bruschetta". Used in crumb form, bread can coat foods, eke out fillings, and protect the surface of food from drying out.

Borlotti, cannellini, black-eyed, kidney and haricot beans are staples throughout Italy (especially in Tuscany), and are used in both hearty soups and simple salads. They are a good source of protein and contain little or no fat.

FISH AND SEAFOOD
All manner of fish and seafood is eaten in Italy, the variety is enormous. Squid, cuttlefish, tuna, swordfish, red mullet, grey mullet, sea bass, sardines, clams, mussels and endless varieties of prawns are popular.

Although you should eat less of the oily fish like sardines, to cut down on calories, there are benefits in fish oil such as their effect on the breakdown of cholesterol.

Anchovies, whether salted or in oil, are used to give a piquant savouriness to some Italian dishes. Salted anchovies are the whole fish (without head) preserved in salt, and need to be rinsed and the backbone removed before using. Anchovies preserved in oil should be rinsed well before using. They are very strong in flavour, so use sparingly.

Fish is often cooked on a barbecue, but it is also steamed, poached, and quickly fried – a non-stick frying pan is good for frying with little or no added fat.

GAME AND MEAT
Game is universally popular – rabbit, hare, wild boar and partridge to name but a few. It is low in fat, free-range, and has lots of taste. Most chicken dishes can be made with all types of game bird, and the flavour will be much stronger. Tuscans often eat meat and balance it with beans and vegetables, whereas Sicilians prefer fish. Beef and veal should be eaten in small quantities, and turkey can

often be substituted for veal. Pork is bred to be lean nowadays and is not so fat ridden as it once was – it is made into all sorts of products, which used judiciously can add a lot of flavour to many different dishes.

HAM AND BACON
Prosciutto is the generic term for ham. Prosciutto crudo is raw cured ham, and Parma ham is a particularly high quality prosciutto crudo. Pancetta is unsmoked Italian bacon, rolled up and sliced to order. It is a dry cure and smoked bacon does not give the same flavour. Cut off as much fat as possible before using these products. Drain off any fat released during cooking if really concerned about cholesterol.

ITALIAN SAUSAGES
These are freshly made with coarsely ground pork, a little fat and highly seasoned with salt and pepper. They are often flavoured with fennel, chilli, basil and pine kernels.

GARLIC
The larger the cloves of garlic, the sweeter it will be. Small hard heads of garlic tend to be bitter and strong. The softer and fresher the garlic, the more subtle the flavour. Avoid mean garlic heads in little boxes! Garlic is used in many ways to give a vast range of flavours.

HERBS
Parsley, basil, sage, rosemary, thyme, bay, mint and oregano are widely used

to enhance flavour without adding calories. Fresh herbs are always better than dried. Capers are the flower bud of the caper plant which grows wild all over Italy. The buds are either salted or preserved in vinegar. The larger seed pods are used too – they add a piquancy to salads and sauces.

SALADS AND VEGETABLES
All kinds of salad leaves, both wild and cultivated, are eaten, and Italian markets spill over with tempting greenery in the summer. Salads are a very important part of the meal, no matter how small the portion – often it is just a few salad leaves to cleanse the palate. They are very often quite bitter leaves like arugula, radicchio, batavia, cos and chicory.

Popular vegetables in Italy are beans, squashes, aubergine (eggplant), fennel, courgettes (zucchini) and their flowers, which can be stuffed, potatoes, and peppers (capsicums).

TOMATOES
Although relative newcomers to Italian cuisine, tomatoes have become an essential ingredient. Fresh tomatoes should be slightly soft, bright red and sweet. Canned and bottled tomatoes are essential in the winter when fresh are not available. Sun-dried tomatoes are used sparingly in Italian cooking. Tomato purée (paste) adds richness and Sicilian "strattu", a clay-like sun-dried concentrate of tomatoes, is a real find – a little goes a long way.

WILD MUSHROOMS
The most famous and much-prized mushroom is the "porcini" or "cep" or "Penny Bun". It is gathered in the wild and much coveted. Both fresh and dried are expensive, but one or two dried mushrooms (after soaking) add great flavour to risottos and sauces, and are very low in fat.

OLIVES
Olives are a much prized crop, picked late in the year when green, or left to ripen on the tree until black or purple. Olive oil is synonymous with Italian cuisine, and the choice is limitless. Choose a cold-pressed fruity, extra virgin olive oil with a low acidity (less than 1%) for dressing salads, and a lighter less expensive oil for cooking and baking. A dark green olive oil does not necessarily guarantee quality – taste it and see. Olive pastes are rich

and salty and can be used sparingly as toppings, bread and pasta flavourings or even whisked into a dressing. Olive oil has a high fat content, but is mono-saturated fat which is healthier than animal fats. Use it in moderation to enhance the flavour of foods. It is good with lemon juice and vinegar.

BALSAMIC VINEGAR

This rich sweet vinegar is made from fermented Trebbiano grapes, aged in oak casks for at least 4 years (and some vinegars for much longer). It is a boon to lighter cooking as it lends a subtle richness to a dish without the fat! There is no real substitute, but sherry vinegar is the nearest thing. Balsamic vinegar is especially good sprinkled over strawberries.

PASTA

Egg pasta is traditionally made with Italian "00" flour (Farina Tipo 00) – the finest, whitest grade of Italian "grano tenero" or soft grain flour, eggs, olive oil and salt. The "00" flour is sometimes mixed with "semolino di grano duro" or semolina flour. This is made from the heart of the wheat, has a high gluten content and is the flour used for making commercial dried pasta. Most commercially dried pasta is made from "grano duro" or hard-wheat or semolina flour and water. This contains much less cholestorol than "pasta al'uovo" made with eggs.

Semolina flour gives dried pasta a firmer texture. It is also good for "flouring" fresh pasta as it is coarser

than flour, aerates it prior to cooking, and does not stick to the pasta during cooking.

Pasta is very versatile and is great value for money as far as satisfying hunger is concerned. In Italy, the pasta is tossed in the sauce to just coat, along with a little of the cooking water, which helps to emulsify the sauce. It is never swamped in sauce, just flavoured with it.

Pasta is essentially a food of the poor, cheap while satisfying hunger and providing a good source of slow and constantly released energy. It contains more carbohydrate and protein than potatoes.

Wholewheat pasta is not eaten much in Italy, but it is extremely nutritious and slightly lower in calories than ordinary dried pasta. Buy good quality pasta – dried pasta is often better than fresh. Eaten in moderation, it can liven up your diet.

FLOUR

Italian breads such as focaccia are made with ordinary plain flour; strong flour makes the dough too elastic and gives the wrong texture.

POLENTA FLOUR (Farina Giallo)

This coarsely ground maize is used for making soft polenta like mashed potato and the firmer sliced and grilled polenta to serve with grilled and roasted meats. It takes about 40 minutes to cook, but "quick cook" or "instant" polenta, which is ready in 5-10 minutes, is a good substitute.

RICE

Arborio rice for risotto is the most widely available exported Italian rice. It is a short grain rice with good absorption and is essential for making creamy risottos. It is the fat and cheese in risottos that make them calorific, not the rice itself, which is very nutritious.

FRUIT AND NUTS

Italians love fruit, whether served raw, cooked or in a salad. Best of all, fruit is eaten with great gusto in sorbets and ice creams. Sorbets are good for a healthy diet as they contain little fat and, served in small quantities, are very refreshing. They were one of the many Arab contributions to Italian cuisine.

Lemons, oranges, watermelon, melon, apricots, peaches, pears, apples, nectarines, plums, persimmon (sharon fruit/kaki fruit), wild strawberries, raspberries, grapes, fresh walnuts, hazelnuts, chestnuts, and almonds are some of the wide choice available to Italians. Preserved fruits such as candied citrus peel are widely used in desserts, baking and sweets.

Almonds, walnuts and hazelnuts are extensively used in Italian desserts and sweets, but have been kept to a minimum in the recipes in this book to reduce calories. Pine kernels, the seeds of pine cones, are expensive as their extraction is labour-intensive. They are generally not toasted, but are quite high in calories, so use them sparingly.

DAIRY PRODUCTS

Cheeses and dairy products are used widely in Northern Italian cooking, quite lavishly. Try to use low or reduced fat versions where possible. Use half-fat or skimmed milk and whipping cream instead of double cream. Low-fat yogurts or fromage frais or blanc are good substitutes for creamy, melting cheeses.

Fresh mozzarella is a favourite for salads and pizzas. The best is made from water buffalo milk. It melts to a delicious stringiness when heated. Use the low-fat makes on the market. Parmigiano (Parmesan) is a hard "grana" cheese. It is salty and crumbly, and a pale straw colour. Parmigiano Reggiano is the best, but Grana Padano is good in cooking. Shaving fine curls of Parmesan onto salads is a current fashion. Although high in fat, a little goes a long way.

Mascarpone is a fresh thick cheese made from cream, and mainly used in desserts – curd cheese mixed with low-fat Greek yogurt could be substituted. Ricotta is a cheese made from whey and should be snowy white and sweet. Reduced-fat ricotta is used in the recipes in this book.

EGGS

Free range farm eggs in Italy have amazingly bright yellow yolks – a result of corn-feeding – and make wonderful yellow omelettes and pasta. Try to limit your intake of eggs as the yolks have a high cholesterol and fat content.

SPICES AND FLOWER WATERS

The Romans used fennel and poppyseeds to flavour breads, but it was in the Renaissance, when the Venetians were the centre of the spice trade with the East, that spices became widely used. Saffron, cinnamon, nutmeg, vanilla, aniseed, cloves, black and white pepper, mace and ginger were used to mask the taste of rotting food, and as preservatives. Orange flower water and rosewater were brought to Sicily by the Arabs and feature heavily in sweets and desserts.

WINE

Enjoying Italian food without wine would be almost sacrilegious, and there is no reason why some wine should not be part of your healthy, low-fat diet. Many sauces and desserts contain wine in modest amounts.

TUSCAN BEAN SOUP

225 g (8 oz) dried white beans (haricot, cannellini),
  soaked overnight
2 tablespoons chopped fresh sage or rosemary
5 tablespoons olive oil
2 cloves garlic, finely chopped
salt and freshly ground pepper
2 cloves garlic, finely sliced
1 fresh red chilli, cored, seeded and chopped
chopped fresh parsley, to garnish

Preheat oven to 170C (325F/Gas 3). Drain
beans and place in a flameproof casserole.
Cover with water to a depth of 5 cm (2 in)
above the beans.

Bring to boil, cover tightly and bake in the
oven for about 1 hour or until tender.
Remove from the oven and allow to cool
slightly in the cooking liquid. Place half the
beans and liquid in a food processor or
blender and process until smooth. Stir into
the beans in the casserole with the sage or
rosemary. Add extra water if too thick. Heat
2 tablespoons olive oil in a frying pan and fry
the chopped garlic until soft and golden. Stir
it into the soup, reheat until boiling, then
simmer gently for 10 minutes.

Taste the soup and season well with salt and
pepper. Heat remaining olive oil in the frying pan and fry the sliced garlic and the
chilli until golden. Pour soup into soup
plates or bowls, spoon garlic and chilli over
the top and sprinkle with chopped parsley.
Serve at once.

Serves 6.

Total Cals/Kj: 1185/4958   Total fat: 60 g
Cals/Kj per portion: 198/826   Fat per portion: 10 g

PASTA & BEAN SOUP

185 g (6 oz/1 cup) dried haricot beans, soaked
  overnight
2 cloves garlic, crushed
1.7 litres (3 pints/7½ cups) chicken stock or water
115 g (4 oz/¼ cup) medium pasta shells
4 tomatoes, skinned, seeded and chopped
4 tablespoons chopped fresh parsley
salt and freshly ground pepper

Drain beans and place in a saucepan with
garlic and chicken stock or water. Simmer,
half-covered, for 2-2½ hours or until tender.

Allow to cool slightly, then transfer beans
and cooking liquid to a food processor or
blender and purée. Return purée to the pan,
add pasta and tomatoes and simmer gently
for 15 minutes until tender. (Add a little
extra chicken stock or water if the soup
looks too thick.)

Stir in chopped parsley and season well with
salt and pepper. Serve at once.

Serves 6.

Total Cals/Kj: 1045/4372   Total fat: 7.3 g
Cals/Kj per portion: 174/729   Fat per portion: 1.2 g

MINESTRONE

2 tablespoons olive oil
55 g (2 oz) lightly smoked streaky bacon, diced
2 large onions, peeled and sliced
2 garlic cloves, skinned and crushed
2 medium carrots, peeled and diced
3 sticks celery, trimmed and sliced
250 g (9 oz/1¼ cups) dried haricot beans, soaked
450 g can chopped tomatoes
2.3 litres (4 pints/10 cups) beef stock
115 g (4 oz) frozen peas
350 g (12 oz) potatoes, peeled and diced
175 g (6 oz) small pasta shapes
225 g (8 oz) green cabbage, thinly sliced
175 g (6 oz) green beans, topped, tailed and sliced
3 tablespoons each chopped fresh parsley and basil
salt and freshly ground pepper

Heat oil in a large saucepan and add bacon, onions, and garlic. Cover and cook gently for 5 minutes, stirring occasionally until soft but not coloured. Add carrots and celery and cook for 2-3 minutes until softening. Drain beans and add to the pan with tomatoes and stock. Cover and simmer for 1-1½ hours, until beans are nearly tender.

Add peas and potatoes and cook for a further 15 minutes, then add the pasta, cabbage, beans and chopped parsley and cook for a further 15 minutes. Stir in the basil, adjust seasoning and serve.

Serves 8.

Total Cals/Kj: 2488/10409   Total fat: 57.4 g
Cals/Kj per portion: 311/1301   Fat per portion: 7.2 g

Note: Serve with freshly grated Parmesan cheese, if wished.

COURGETTE SOUP

2 tablespoons olive or sunflower oil
2 medium sweet onions, finely chopped
1.4 litres (2½ pints/6¼ cups) chicken stock
900 g (2 lb) courgettes (zucchini), trimmed and
  grated
fresh lemon juice, to taste
salt and freshly ground pepper
2 tablespoons chopped fresh chervil or tarragon
150 ml (5 fl oz/⅔ cup) low-fat Greek yogurt, to
  serve

Heat oil in a large saucepan and add onions.
Cover and cook gently for about 20 minutes
until they are very soft but not coloured,
stirring occasionally.

Pour in stock and bring to the boil. Stir in
courgettes (zucchini) and bring to the boil
again then turn down the heat and simmer
for 15 minutes. Season to taste with lemon
juice, salt and pepper.

Stir in chopped chervil or tarragon, add a
swirl of yogurt and serve at once.

Serves 6.

Total Cals/Kj: 497/2079   Total fat: 26.9 g
Cals/Kj per portion: 83/346   Fat per portion: 4.5 g

──ROASTED PEPPER SOUP──

6 yellow peppers (capsicums)
4 medium leeks, white and pale green parts only,
   thinly sliced
2 tablespoons olive oil
685 ml (1¼ pints/3 cups) chicken stock
salt and freshly ground pepper
toasted country bread, to serve

Preheat oven to 240C (475F/Gas 9). Place peppers (capsicums) in a large roasting pan and roast in the oven for 20-30 minutes until they begin to char, turning once. Remove from oven and place in a polythene bag, closing tightly. Leave for 10 minutes.

Meanwhile, place sliced leeks in a bowl of cold water to soak for 5 minutes. Remove peppers (capsicums) from the bag and scrape off skins. Pull out the stalks and the seeds should come with them. Halve the peppers (capsicums), scrape out any remaining seeds and roughly chop the flesh. Drain the leeks.

Heat oil, add leeks and cook them gently for 10 minutes until soft but not coloured. Add peppers (capsicums), stock and season with salt and pepper. Bring to the boil then turn down the heat and simmer for 20 minutes. Purée in a blender, then pass through a sieve into the rinsed-out pan. Reheat, taste and season. Serve with toasted country bread.

Serves 4.

Total Cals/Kj: 573/2397   Total fat: 26.1 g
Cals/Kj per portion: 143/599   Fat per portion: 6.5 g

PUMPKIN SOUP

700 g (1½ lb) fresh pumpkin
6 cloves garlic, unpeeled
4 tablespoons olive oil
2 medium leeks, finely sliced and washed
1 stick celery, chopped
55 g (2 oz/¼ cup) long grain white rice
1.4 litres (50 fl oz/6¼ cups) vegetable or chicken
  stock or water
salt and freshly ground pepper
4 tablespoons chopped fresh parsley
parsley sprigs, to garnish

Preheat oven to 200C (400F/Gas 6). Scrape out seeds from pumpkin, cut off the skin and cut flesh into large cubes.

Place pumpkin in a roasting pan with garlic cloves and toss with 2 tablespoons olive oil. Do not crowd pan – use 2 tins if necessary. Roast in oven for 30 minutes until tender and beginning to brown. Meanwhile, heat remaining olive oil in a large saucepan, add leeks and celery and cook over gentle heat for 10 minutes until just beginning to brown and soften. Stir in the rice, stock or water, bring to the boil, cover and simmer for about 15-20 minutes until rice is tender.

Remove pumpkin from oven, cool slightly, then pop garlic cloves out of skins. Add the garlic and pumpkin to pan, bring to boil and simmer for 10 minutes. Purée in a blender and return to pan. Season with plenty of black pepper. Add extra stock or water if the soup is too thick. Reheat and stir in chopped parsley. Serve garnished with parsley sprigs.

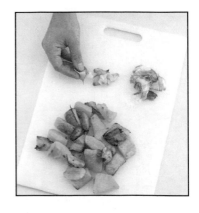

Serves 6.

Total Cals/Kj: 805/3368   Total fat: 49 g
Cals/Kj per portion: 134/561   Fat per portion: 8.3 g

CHICKPEA SOUP

400 g (14 oz/2 cups) dried chickpeas, soaked
  overnight
1 tablespoon chopped fresh rosemary
2 fresh bay leaves
2 cloves garlic, peeled and halved
75 g (3 oz) pancetta or smoked lean streaky bacon,
  chopped
2 medium onions, finely chopped
1 carrot, chopped
1 stick celery, chopped
salt and freshly ground black pepper
rosemary sprigs, to garnish

Drain chickpeas, place in a saucepan with
the rosemary, bay and garlic.

Cover with fresh water and bring to the boil.
Cover pan and simmer chickpeas for about
40 minutes until tender. Meanwhile, heat a
non-stick frying pan, add pancetta or bacon
and fry over medium heat until fat begins to
run. Add chopped vegetables and cook for
5-10 minutes until they are beginning to
soften and brown.

Drain chickpeas, reserve cooking liquid and
return pulses to the pan. Stir in pancetta and
vegetables and enough of reserved cooking
liquid to cover. Bring to the boil, half-cover,
turn down heat and simmer chickpeas for
30 minutes until starting to disintegrate and
thicken the soup, stirring occasionally. Taste
and season. Serve garnished with rosemary.

Serves 6.

Total Cals/Kj: 698/2946   Total fat: 18.1 g
Cals/Kj per portion: 116/491   Fat per portion: 3 g

PAPPA AL POMODORO

4 tablespoons olive oil
1 onion, finely chopped
3 cloves garlic, finely chopped
1.25 kg (2¾ lb) very ripe tomatoes, chopped
1.5 litres (53 fl oz/6¼ cups) vegetable, chicken or
  meat stock
400 g (14 oz) stale breadcrumbs
55 g (2 oz) fresh basil leaves, shredded
salt and freshly ground black pepper

Heat half the oil in a medium saucepan, add
onion and garlic and fry gently for 5 minutes
until softened. Stir in tomatoes, bring to the
boil and simmer for 10 minutes.

Transfer the mixture to a food processor or
blender and purée. Pass the purée through a
sieve into a large saucepan, then whisk in
the stock.

Slowly bring to boil and stir in breadcrumbs
and half the basil. Season to taste with salt
and pepper. Turn down the heat, cover and
simmer gently for about 45 minutes or until
thick and creamy, stirring occasionally. Stir
in remaining oil and basil, check seasoning
and serve at once.

Serves 8.

Total Cals/Kj: 2141/8957   Total fat: 56 g
Cals/Kj per portion: 268/1119 Fat per portion: 7 g

MUSSEL SOUP

2 tablespoons olive oil
3 cloves garlic, 2 chopped and 1 whole
225 g (8 oz) ripe tomatoes, chopped
pinch of chilli powder
6 slices country bread
450 ml (16 fl oz/3 cups) fish or vegetable stock
1.4 kg (3 lb) mussels, scrubbed and de-bearded
3 tablespoons chopped fresh parsley

Heat the oil in a large flameproof casserole, add chopped garlic and cook until golden. Stir in the tomatoes and chilli powder. Cover and simmer for 25 minutes until the oil separates.

Cut whole garlic clove in half. Toast bread on both sides and rub each side with a cut side of the garlic clove.

Add stock to the casserole and bring to boil. Add mussels, cover and cook for 3-5 minutes until all the mussels are open, occasionally shaking the pan. Scatter parsley over the top and serve with the garlic bread.

Serves 6.

Total Cals/Kj: 1026/4292   Total fat: 38.9 g
Cals/Kj per portion: 171/715   Fat per portion: 6.3 g

Variation: Substitute clams for the mussels.

FENNEL SOUP

55 ml (2 fl oz/¼ cup) olive oil
1 medium onion, chopped
225 g (8 oz) fennel, peeled, cored and thinly sliced,
  reserving any green fronds for garnish
1 potato, diced
685 ml (24 fl oz/3 cups) chicken stock
salt and freshly ground pepper
fresh lemon juice, to taste

Heat oil in a large saucepan and add onion.
Cook for 5 minutes until onion is beginning
to soften. Add fennel and potato and cook
for 5 minutes until fennel begins to soften.

Pour in chicken stock and bring to boil.
Turn down heat, cover and simmer for about
45 minutes. Purée in a blender and pass it
through a sieve into the rinsed-out pan.

Reheat soup, taste and season well with salt,
pepper and lemon juice. Garnish with the
reserved fennel fronds and serve at once.

Serves 6.

Total Cals/Kj: 556/2326   Total fat: 39.7 g
Cals/Kj per portion: 93/387   Fat per portion: 6.6 g

—PEPPERS WITH ARTICHOKES—

6 red, orange or yellow peppers (capsicums)
12 frozen artichoke hearts, thawed or 12 artichokes
  in brine, drained
24 anchovy fillets, drained
6 tablespoons extra virgin olive oil
salt and freshly ground pepper
4 cloves garlic, sliced
2 tablespoons chopped fresh oregano

Preheat grill. Arrange the whole peppers (capsicums) in a grill pan and roast under grill until the skin begins to char. Turn the peppers (capsicums) until they are evenly charred. Slip off the skins while still warm.

Cut peppers (capsicums) in half lengthways and scrape out the seeds. Place the peppers cut side up in a shallow serving dish. Cut the artichoke hearts in half and place two halves in each pepper. Arrange 2 anchovy fillets over each pepper (capsicum) half. Spoon a little olive oil over each artichoke.

Season with salt and pepper, then scatter the sliced garlic and oregano over the top. Cover and refrigerate overnight for the flavours to meld. Allow to come to room temperature before serving with crusty Italian bread.

Serves 6.

Total Cals/Kj: 1762/7373   Total fat: 149 g
Cals/Kj per portion: 294/1228   Fat per portion: 24.9 g

TOMATO BRUSCHETTA

250 g (9 oz) half-fat mozzarella, cut into small cubes
20 ripe cherry tomatoes, quartered
3 tablespoons olive oil
1 teaspoon balsamic or sherry vinegar
salt and freshly ground pepper
6 thick slices country bread
2 garlic cloves, skinned
115 g (4 oz) rocket (arugula) or watercress
generous handful of fresh basil leaves, to garnish

Place mozzarella in a bowl with tomatoes.
Whisk together olive oil and vinegar, season
with salt and pepper and pour it over the
cheese and tomatoes. Mix well.

Toast the bread on both sides and keep it
warm. Cut the garlic cloves in half and rub
each slice of toasted bread with a cut side of
garlic clove.

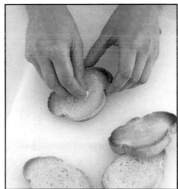

Place a slice of toast on each of 6 plates and
surround each slice with rocket (arugula) or
watercress. Pile the mozzarella and tomato
mixture on top of the toast, garnish with
fresh basil leaves and serve.

Serves 6.

Total Cals/Kj: 1386/5799   Total fat: 76.6 g
Cals/Kj per portion: 231/966   Fat per portion: 12.7 g

—GRILLED PROSCIUTTO & FIGS—

8 fresh ripe figs
3 tablespoons olive oil
12 thin slices of prosciutto or Parma ham
3 tablespoons freshly grated Parmesan cheese
crushed black pepper, to serve

Take each fig and stand it upright. Using a sharp kitchen knife, make 2 cuts across and downwards in each fig not quite quartering it, but keeping it intact. Ease the figs open and brush with olive oil.

Place the figs cut side down on a barbecue or ridged griddle and cook for 5-10 minutes until hot and golden brown, turning once. Alternatively, place under a searing hot grill and grill until browning and hot through. While the figs are cooking, place half the prosciutto slices on the barbecue or griddle and grill for 2-3 minutes until starting to crisp. Remove and keep warm while cooking the remaining slices.

Arrange 3 pieces of the ham and 2 figs per person on warm plates. Sprinkle with grated Parmesan and season with plenty of crushed black pepper. Serve at once.

Serves 4.

Total Cals/Kj: 847/3543   Total fat: 53.7 g
Cals/Kj per portion: 212/886   Fat per portion: 13 g

──CHICKEN LIVER CROSTINI──

225 g (8 oz) fresh chicken livers
2 tablespoons olive oil
2 medium leeks, white parts only, washed and finely
  chopped
1 stick celery, finely chopped
1 tablespoon balsamic or sherry vinegar
2 tablespoons capers in brine, drained
70 ml (2½ fl oz/⅓ cup) chicken stock
1 tablespoon chopped fresh thyme
salt and freshly ground pepper
12 slices of french bread, toasted on both sides
thyme sprigs, to garnish

Wash livers, removing gristle or discoloured bits. Dry on absorbent kitchen paper.

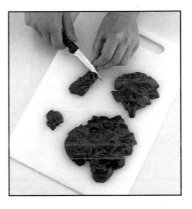

Heat olive oil in a non-stick frying pan, add leeks and celery and cook for 5 minutes until soft but not coloured. Add chicken livers and fry them with the vegetables for about 5 minutes. Sprinkle with the vinegar and allow it to evaporate over the heat.

Stir in the capers, chicken stock and thyme and bring to the boil. Season well with salt and pepper. Turn down the heat and simmer for a further 10-15 minutes until thickened and creamy, stirring all the time. Spread the mixture on the warm toasted bread and serve at once, garnished with thyme sprigs.

Serves 6.

Total Cals/Kj: 1851/7745   Total fat: 50 g
Cals/Kj per portion: 308/1290   Fat per portion: 8.4 g

—PEPPER & ANCHOVY SALAD—

3 large red and 3 large yellow peppers (capsicums)
70 ml (2½ fl oz/⅓ cup) olive oil or olive oil and
sunflower oil mixed
1 tablespoon wine or balsamic vinegar
salt and freshly ground pepper
55 g (2 oz) can anchovies, drained, rinsed and
chopped
115 g (4 oz) black olives, stoned
3-4 tablespoons chopped fresh parsley
2 hard-boiled eggs

Preheat oven to 240C (475F) Gas 9. Place peppers (capsicums) in a large roasting pan and roast in oven for 20-30 minutes until they begin to char, turning once.

Remove peppers (capsicums) from the oven and place in a polythene bag, closing tightly. Leave for 10 minutes, then remove them from the bag and scrape off the skins. Pull out the stalks and the seeds should come with them. Halve peppers (capsicums), scrape out any remaining seeds then cut the flesh into wide strips. Put oil, vinegar, salt and pepper, anchovies, olives and parsley into a large bowl and mix well. Add peppers (capsicums) and toss to coat thoroughly.

Halve eggs and remove yolks. Roughly chop whites and scatter them over the peppers (capsicums). Sieve the yolks and sprinkle them over the whites. Chill before serving.

Serves 6 (or more if served with other antipasti).

Total Cals/Kj: 1138/4761   Total fat: 90.6 g
Cals/Kj per portion: 190/793   Fat per portion: 15 g

GARLIC & LEMON PRAWNS

225 g (8 oz) small to medium raw prawns
salt and freshly ground pepper
4 tablespoons olive oil
2 tablespoons sunflower oil
3 large cloves garlic, coarsely chopped
1 dried red chilli pepper, stem and seeds removed,
  chopped
fresh lemon juice
2 tablespoons chopped fresh parsley
crusty bread, to serve

Shell prawns and pat dry on absorbent
kitchen paper. Lay prawns in a dish and
sprinkle lightly with salt.

Heat the oil in a non-stick frying pan, add
garlic and chilli and fry for 1-2 minutes until
garlic is golden. Immediately add prawns
and cook over high heat for 2 minutes until
the prawns are just tender. Add lemon juice
to taste and check the seasoning.

Stir in chopped fresh parsley, then serve the
prawns in ramekins, hot or cold with plenty
of crusty bread.

Serves 4.

Total Cals/Kj: 775/3242   Total fat: 67 g
Cals/Kj per portion: 194/810 Fat per portion: 16.9 g

PANZANELLA

200 g (7 oz) country bread, crusts removed and
cubed
6 ripe tomatoes, roughly chopped
1 red onion, chopped
½ cucumber, seeds removed and cubed
2 sticks celery, sliced
4 tablespoons olive oil
1 tablespoon wine vinegar
salt and freshly ground pepper
55 g (2 oz) fresh basil, torn

Place bread cubes in a bowl and sprinkle
lightly with just enough water to moisten
them. Leave to stand for 5 minutes.

Add all the vegetables to the bread and toss
until well mixed. Sprinkle with the oil and
vinegar and season with salt and pepper.
Toss again.

Add basil and toss the salad. Transfer to a
serving bowl and leave to stand in a cool
place for 20 minutes; do not leave it longer
or the salad will go mushy. Serve at room
temperature.

Serves 6.

Total Cals/Kj: 1039/4347   Total fat: 50.4 g
Cals/Kj per portion: 173/724   Fat per portion: 8.4 g

TUNA & CAPER PÂTÉ

200 g (7 oz) can tuna in brine or water, drained
4 tablespoons low-fat ricotta or curd cheese
grated rind of 1 lemon
2 tablespoons freshly squeezed lemon juice
2 tablespoons olive oil
1 tablespoon capers in brine, drained and rinsed
1 clove garlic, finely chopped
1 teaspoon chopped fresh thyme
salt and freshly ground black pepper
toasted bread or prepared raw vegetables, to serve
thyme sprigs, to garnish (optional)

Place the tuna in a bowl and mash with a fork. Beat in the ricotta, lemon rind, lemon juice, olive oil, capers, garlic and thyme until creamy. Taste and season with salt and pepper.

To serve, spread the pâté on slices of toasted bread. Alternatively, serve it as a dip with a selection of raw vegetables. Garnish with thyme sprigs, if wished.

Serves 4.

Total Cals/Kj: 462/1933   Total fat: 25.9 g
Cals/Kj per portion: 115/483   Fat per portion: 6.5 g

BEAN & BEEF SALAD

450 g (1 lb) fresh young unshelled broad beans
6 slices Bresaola (Italian dry cured beef fillet)
115 g (4 oz) pecorino cheese
2 tablespoons olive oil
1 tablespoon freshly squeezed lemon juice
1 teaspoon chopped fresh oregano
2 tablespoons chopped fresh parsley
pinch dried red pepper flakes
salt and freshly ground pepper

Remove broad beans from their shells and blanch in boiling water for 20 seconds. Drain, refresh in cold water and pop the beans out of their skins. Place in a bowl.

Cube the pecorino cheese and cut the beef into strips. Add to the beans in the bowl.

Add olive oil, lemon juice, oregano, parsley and pepper flakes. Toss together, taste and adjust the seasoning. Serve immediately.

Serves 6.

Total Cals/Kj: 1115/4665   Total fat: 68 g
Cals/Kj per portion: 186/777   Fat per portion: 11.3 g

Variation: Instead of fresh beans, use 175 g (6 oz) thawed frozen broad beans. Do not blanch, simply pop them out of their skins.

—TUNA, BEAN & ONION SALAD —

175 g (6 oz) dried white haricot or cannellini beans,
  soaked overnight
2 tablespoons olive oil
1 tablespoon sunflower oil
1 teaspoon balsamic vinegar
salt and freshly ground pepper
1 small red onion, finely sliced
1 leek, white and light green parts finely sliced
1 tablespoon chopped fresh parsley
200 g (7 oz) can tuna fish in brine, drained
1 tablespoon chopped fresh chives

Drain and rinse beans. Place in a saucepan
and cover with cold water.

Bring to the boil, turn down the heat, cover
and simmer for 1–1½ hours or until beans are
tender but not falling apart. Drain. Whisk
together the oils, vinegar, salt and pepper
and mix into the hot beans.

Stir in the onion, leek, parsley and then the
tuna fish, being careful not to break up the
fish too much. Allow to cool, then transfer
mixture to a serving dish, sprinkle with the
chopped chives and serve.

Serves 4.

Total Cals/Kj: 1048/4384   Total fat: 37.8 g
Cals/Kj per portion: 262/1096   Fat per portion: 9.4 g

BASIC EGG PASTA

200 g (7 oz/1¾ cups) plain white flour
pinch of salt
2 large eggs, beaten
1 teaspoon olive oil

To make pasta by hand, sift flour and salt onto a clean surface and make a well in the centre. Beat eggs and oil together and pour into well. Gradually mix eggs into flour with the fingers of one hand. Knead the pasta for about 10 minutes until smooth, wrap and allow to rest for at least 30 minutes before rolling out by hand or machine.

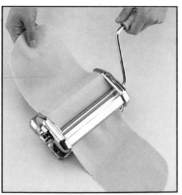

Or, put ingredients in a food processor and process until dough begins to come together. Tip out and knead for 10 minutes until smooth. Wrap in cling film and rest for 30 minutes, then roll out on a lightly floured surface until thin enough to read newsprint through it. Alternatively, to roll out in a pasta machine, feed dough several times through widest setting first, then pass pasta through machine, reducing settings until reaching right thickness. Generally, second from last setting is best for tagliatelle; the finest for ravioli or pasta to be filled.

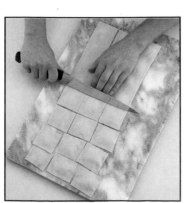

Hang the pasta over a broom handle to dry slightly (ravioli should be made at once as it needs to be slightly sticky). Pass the pasta through chosen cutters and transfer to a tray covered with a clean tea towel sprinkled with a little flour. Toss pasta lightly in the flour and use as soon as possible. Or, drape pasta over broom handle until ready to cook.

Serves 4.

Total Cals/Kj: 893/3736   Total fat: 19.1 g
Cals/Kj per portion: 223/934   Fat per portion: 4.8 g

PASTA NAPOLETANA

900 g (2 lb) fresh ripe red tomatoes, or two 400 g
  (14 oz) cans plum tomatoes with juice, chopped
1 medium onion, finely chopped
1 medium carrot, finely diced
1 stick celery, diced
150 ml (5 fl oz/⅔ cup) dry white wine (optional)
parsley sprig
salt and freshly ground pepper
pinch of sugar
1 tablespoon chopped fresh oregano
350 g (12 oz) dried pasta of your choice
freshly grated Parmesan cheese, to serve (optional)

Put vegetables, wine, parsley, seasoning and
sugar in a medium saucepan.

Bring to the boil and simmer, half-covered
for 45 minutes until very thick, stirring
occasionally. Pass mixture through a sieve or
mouli-legumes, or purée in a blender and
sieve to remove the tomato seeds. Stir in the
chopped oregano, then taste and adjust the
seasoning, if necessary. Reheat gently.

Bring a large pan of salted water to the boil
and cook pasta according to manufacturer's
instructions until *al dente* (tender but firm to
the bite). Drain well and toss with the hot
sauce. Serve at once, with grated Parmesan
cheese if wished.

Serves 4.

Total Cals/Kj: 1529/6397   Total fat: 9.4 g
Cals/Kj per portion: 382/1599 Fat per portion: 2.4 g

—SPAGHETTI WITH GARLIC—

5 tablespoons olive oil
salt and freshly ground pepper
2 cloves garlic, finely chopped
1 red chilli. seeded and chopped
400 g (14 oz) dried spaghettini or spaghetti
2 tablespoons chopped fresh parsley

Heat oil in a medium saucepan. Add garlic and a pinch of salt and cook very gently until golden, stirring all the time. Do not allow the garlic to become too brown or it will taste bitter. Add chopped chilli and cook for 1 minute.

Bring a large pan of salted water to the boil and cook pasta according to manufacturer's instructions until *al dente* (tender but firm to the bite). Drain well.

Toss pasta with the warm, not sizzling, garlic and chilli oil and add plenty of black pepper and the parsley. Serve immediately.

Serves 6.

Total Cals/Kj: 1862/7857   Total fat: 62 g
Cals/Kj per portion: 310/1309   Fat per portion: 10 g

PASTA CARBONARA

115 g (4 oz) smoked lean streaky bacon or pancetta
in a piece
1 clove garlic, finely chopped
300 g (10 oz) dried spaghetti or other ribbon pasta
3 eggs, beaten
salt and freshly ground pepper
3 tablespoons freshly grated Parmesan cheese

Cut bacon into dice and place in a medium saucepan with the garlic. Place over the heat and fry in its own fat until brown. Keep warm.

Bring a large saucepan of salted water to boil and cook pasta according to manufacturer's instructions until *al dente* (tender but still firm to the bite). Drain well. Quickly turn the spaghetti into the pan with the bacon.

Stir in eggs, a little salt, lots of pepper and half the cheese. Toss well to mix. The eggs should lightly cook with the heat from the spaghetti. Serve in warm bowls with the remaining cheese.

Serves 4.

Total Cals/Kj: 1576/6672   Total fat: 40 g
Cals/Kj per portion: 394/1668   Fat per portion: 10 g

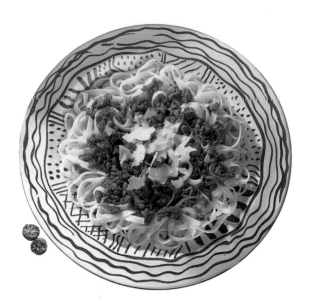

PASTA BOLOGNESE

75 g (3 oz) pancetta or bacon in a piece, diced
1 medium onion, finely chopped
1 medium carrot, finely diced
1 celery stick, finely chopped
225 g (8 oz) lean minced beef
115 g (4 oz) chicken livers, trimmed and chopped
1 medium potato, grated
2 tablespoons tomato purée (paste)
115 ml (4 fl oz/½ cup) white wine
200 ml (7 fl oz/1 cup) beef stock or water
salt and freshly ground pepper
freshly grated nutmeg
400 g (14 oz) dried spaghetti, fettuccine or tagliatelle
freshly grated Parmesan cheese, to serve (optional)

Heat a saucepan and add pancetta. Cook in its own fat for 2-3 minutes until browning. Add onion, carrot and celery and brown them. Stir in minced beef and brown over high heat, breaking it up with a wooden spoon. Stir in the chicken livers and cook them for 2-3 minutes.

Add potato, tomato purée (paste), mix well and pour in wine and stock. Season with salt, pepper and nutmeg. Bring to boil, half-cover and simmer for 35 minutes until reduced and thickened, stirring occasionally. Meanwhile, cook pasta in boiling salted water until tender. Drain well and toss with sauce. Serve with Parmesan cheese, if liked.

Serves 6.

Total Cals/Kj: 2233/9453   Total fat: 37.9 g
Cals/Kj per portion: 372/1575   Fat per portion: 6 g

—PUMPKIN RAVIOLI IN BROTH—

450 g (1 lb) fresh pumpkin, skin on but seeds
  removed, thickly sliced
2 egg yolks
40 g (1½ oz) freshly grated Parmesan cheese
5 fresh sage leaves, chopped
½ teaspoon salt
pinch of freshly grated nutmeg
2 quantities Basic Egg Pasta Dough (see page 32)
beaten egg for brushing
850 ml (30 fl oz/3¾ cups) hot strong chicken stock
extra sage leaves, to garnish

Preheat oven to 350 F (180 C) Gas 4. Boil
pumpkin in salted water for 20 minutes until
soft. Drain well and place on a baking sheet.

Bake in oven for 10-15 minutes to dry out
but not brown. Scoop flesh from the skin,
cool, then mash with egg yolks, cheese, sage,
salt and nutmeg. Spoon into a piping bag.
Halve dough and wrap one half in cling film.
Roll other piece thinly to a rectangle on a
lightly floured surface. Cover with a clean
damp tea towel and repeat with the remaining pasta. Pipe small mounds of filling in
even rows, spacing them at 4 cm (1½ in)
intervals across one piece of the dough.
With a pastry brush, brush the spaces of
dough between the mounds with beaten egg.

Lift remaining pasta over filling. Press down
between pockets of filling. Cut into squares
with a serrated cutter or sharp knife, transfer
to a floured tea towel and rest for 1 hour.
Bring a large saucepan of salted water to the
boil. Toss in ravioli and cook for 3 minutes
until puffy, then drain well. Serve with the
hot stock, garnished with sage leaves.

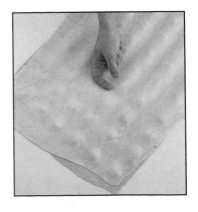

Serves 6.

Total Cals/Kj: 2137/9017   Total fat: 63.7 g
Cals/Kj per portion: 356/1503   Fat per portion: 10.6 g

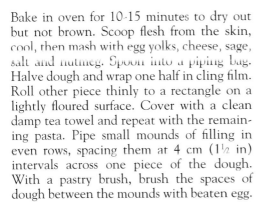

TAGLIATELLE TRAPANESE

3 ripe tomatoes
4 garlic cloves, chopped
salt and freshly ground black pepper
55 g (2 oz) fresh basil leaves
75 g (3 oz) blanched almonds
5 tablespoons olive and sunflower oil, mixed
2 quantities Basic Egg Pasta Dough (see page 32)
extra chopped fresh tomatoes, to garnish

Place all the ingredients except pasta and garnish in a food processor and purée until smooth. Chill in the refrigerator.

Roll out pasta as thinly as possible. Dust with flour and roll up into a sausage shape. Using a sharp knife, cut pasta into 0.5 cm (¼ in) slices. Unravel and place on a floured tea towel until ready to cook.

Bring a large pan of boiling salted water to the boil. Throw in the pasta and cook it for 2-3 minutes, drain well and toss the pasta with the tomato pesto. Serve immediately with extra chopped tomatoes as a garnish.

Serves 8.

Total Cals/Kj: 2990/12568   Total fat: 127 g
Cals/Kj per portion: 374/1571   Fat per portion: 15 g

──ONION & ANCHOVY PIZZA──

15 g (½ oz) fresh yeast, 15 ml (1 tbsp) dried active
  baking yeast, or 7 g (¼ oz) sachet easy-blend yeast
pinch of sugar
350 g (12 oz/3 cups) strong plain white bread flour
1 tablespoon olive oil
½ teaspoon salt
FOR THE TOPPING :
1 tablespoon olive oil and sunflower oil, mixed
900 g (2 lb) red onions, thinly sliced
2 tablespoons freshly squeezed lemon juice
2 tablespoons chopped fresh oregano and rosemary
8 anchovy fillets in oil, drained, rinsed and sliced
  lengthways if wished, or 6 anchovies in salt, boned
  and rinsed
10 black olives, stoned
rosemary sprigs, to garnish

In a bowl, cream fresh yeast with sugar and
whisk in 250 ml (9 fl oz/1 cup) warm water.
Leave 10 minutes. Use dried yeast, according to packet instructions. Sift flour into a
bowl and make well in centre. Pour in yeast,
oil and salt; mix until dough comes together.
On a floured surface, knead 10 minutes until
smooth. Place in a clean oiled bowl, cover
with damp tea towel and leave to rise until
doubled in size. To make topping, heat oil in
a pan and stir in onions and lemon juice.
Cover and cook over gentle heat until
onions are soft. Add chopped herbs.

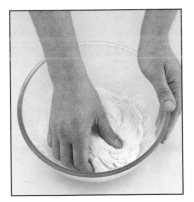

Preheat oven to 240C (475F/Gas 9). Knock
back dough and stretch out to 30 cm (12 in)
circle on a floured baking sheet. Spread
onions evenly over the dough and scatter
with anchovy fillets and olives. Bake in oven
for 10-15 minutes until crisp and golden,
scattering the rosemary sprigs over the top
for the last 3 minutes. Serve with salad.

Serves 6.

Total Cals/Kj: 1886/7947   Total fat: 41.6 g
Cals/Kj per portion: 314/1325 Fat per portion: 6.9 g

PIZZA MARGHERITA

15 g (½ oz) fresh yeast, 15 ml (1 tbsp) dried active
  baking yeast, or 7 g (¼ oz) sachet easy-blend yeast
pinch of sugar
350 g (12 oz) strong plain white bread flour, plus
  extra for dusting
3 tablespoons olive oil
½ teaspoon salt
8 tablespoons passata
115 g (4 oz) half-fat mozzarella cheese, thinly sliced
pinch of dried oregano
fresh basil leaves, shredded
salt and freshly ground black pepper

In a bowl, cream fresh yeast with sugar and
whisk in 250 ml (9 fl oz/1 cup) warm water.
Leave for 10 minutes until frothy. For dried
yeasts, follow the packet instructions. Sift
flour into a large bowl and make a well in
centre. Pour in yeast mixture, oil and salt.
Mix together with a round-bladed knife,
then hands until the dough comes together.
Tip out onto a floured surface and knead for
10 minutes until smooth and elastic. Place
dough in a clean oiled bowl, cover with a
damp tea towel and leave to rise for about
1 hour until doubled in size.

Preheat oven to 240C (475F/Gas 9). Knock
back dough and roll out, or stretch with your
fingers, to a 30 cm (12 in) circle on a large
floured baking sheet. Spread passata over the
dough, avoiding the edges. Scatter cheese,
herbs, salt and pepper over the surface.
Drizzle with oil. Bake for 10-15 minutes
until golden and crisp. Serve with salad.

Serves 4.

Total Cals/Kj: 1719/7192   Total fat: 49.7 g
Cals/Kj per portion: 286/1198   Fat per portion: 7.9 g

SAUSAGE RAGU WITH POLENTA

450 g (1 lb) fresh Italian sausages
1 tablespoon olive oil
1 medium onion, chopped
450 ml (16 fl oz/2 cups) passata (strained tomatoes)
150 ml (5 fl oz/⅔ cup) dry red wine
6 sun-dried tomatoes, soaked in hot water then
    sliced
salt and freshly ground pepper
300 g (11 oz) quick-cook polenta
freshly grated Parmesan cheese (optional), to serve

Squeeze sausagemeat out of skins into a bowl and break up the meat. Heat oil in a medium saucepan and add chopped onion. Cook for 5 minutes until soft and golden.

Stir in sausagemeat and brown it all over, breaking up the lumps with a wooden spoon. Pour in passata and wine and bring to the boil. Add sun-dried tomatoes and simmer for 30 minutes or until well reduced, stirring occasionally. Season with salt and pepper. Meanwhile, bring 1.4 litre (50 fl oz/6¾ cups) water to the boil in a pan with 2 teaspoons salt, then sprinkle in the polenta, stirring or whisking to prevent lumps forming. Simmer for 5-10 minutes according to the packet instructions, until polenta has thickened like soft mashed potato, stirring constantly.

Spoon the polenta into 6 large soup plates and make a dip in the centre of each. Top with the sausage ragu and serve at once, with grated Parmesan cheese if wished.

Serves 6.

Total Cals/Kj: 2326/9722   Total fat: 79 g
Cals/Kj per portion: 388/1620   Fat per portion: 13 g

Note: If you can't buy fresh Italian sausages, use good quality sausages mixed with a little crushed garlic, black pepper and fennel.

SEAFOOD & SAFFRON RISOTTO

two 0.4 g sachets of saffron threads
1.4 litres (50 fl oz/6¼ cups) fish stock
300 ml (10 fl oz/1¼ cups) dry white wine
350 g (12 oz) raw headless shell-on prawns
6 baby squid, cleaned and cut into rings
6 fresh scallops
225 g (8 oz) fresh venus (baby) clams, rinsed
450 g (1 lb) fresh mussels, cleaned
1 medium onion, peeled and chopped
350 g (12 oz) risotto (arborio) rice
3 tablespoons chopped fresh parsley, to garnish

Place the saffron in a small bowl and cover with boiling water. Leave to infuse while you cook the fish.

Bring stock and wine to simmering point, add prawns; cook for 2 minutes. Add squid and scallops and cook 2 minutes. Remove fish with a slotted spoon and set aside. Add clams and mussels to stock, bring to boil, and cover. Cook for 3-5 minutes until opened. Remove and set aside. Place 3 tablespoons stock in a large pan and add onion. Cook gently for 5 minutes until softened and the stock has evaporated. Stir in rice and cook for 2 minutes until rice looks milky. Add saffron water and a ladleful of stock and simmer until absorbed, stirring.

Continue adding the stock, ladle by ladle, until all but 2 ladlefuls is added, and the rice is tender but still has some bite to it. (This should take about 20 minutes.) Season well. Stir in the remaining stock and seafood and cook gently with the lid on for 5 minutes or until piping hot. Transfer to a warmed bowl and sprinkle with parsley. Serve at once.

Serves 6.

Total Cals/Kj: 2406/10199   Total fat: 16 g
Cals/Kj per portion: 400/1700   Fat per portion: 2.7 g

SICILIAN SARDINES

18 fresh sardines
55 g (2 oz) pine nuts, toasted
55 g (2 oz) raisins
3 tablespoons chopped fresh parsley
finely grated rind and juice of 1 orange
salt and freshly ground black pepper
bay leaves
115 ml (4 fl oz/½ cup) olive oil

Scale sardines and cut off heads. Slit open the bellies and remove the guts under cold running water. Slide your thumb along the backbone to release flesh along its length. Hold backbone at head end and lift it out.

Preheat oven to 180C (350F/Gas 4). Mix together pine nuts, raisins, parsley, orange rind and salt and pepper. Place a spoonful on the flesh-side of each fish. Roll up from the head end and secure with a wooden cocktail stick, if necessary.

Place the fish in an oiled ovenproof dish so that they are tightly packed together with the tails sticking up. Tuck a few bay leaves between them. Pour over the orange juice and olive oil over them, season well and bake in the oven for 10 minutes. Remove cocktail sticks and serve sardines hot or cold with a tomato and onion salad.

Serves 6.

Total Cals/Kj: 1605/6715   Total fat:139 g
Cals/Kj per portion: 267/1119   Fat per portion: 23 g

─SQUID WITH AUBERGINES─

2 cloves garlic, finely chopped
2 tablespoons olive oil
juice of 1 lemon
1 teaspoon sweet chilli sauce
2 small red chillies, seeded and chopped
700 g (1½ lb) baby squid, cleaned, tubes and
  tentacles separated
vegetable oil for brushing
2 medium aubergines (eggplants), very thinly sliced
115 g (4 oz) rocket (arugula)
lemon wedges, to serve

In a bowl, mix together garlic, olive oil, lemon juice, chilli sauce and chillies.

Stir squid into marinade, cover and leave to marinate for 2 hours. Heat a griddle until smoking and brush with oil. Grill aubergine (eggplant) slices in batches for 2 minutes on each side. Transfer to a warm oven to keep warm. Remove squid from marinade and reserve the marinade.

Heat griddle until searing hot and fry squid for about 20 seconds on each side, then transfer to a plate. Pour marinade into a pan and heat gently. Arrange aubergine (eggplant) slices on 4 warm plates. Pile the squid on top and spoon over a little marinade. Surround each portion with a ring of rocket leaves. Serve at once, with lemon wedges.

Serves 4.

Total Cals/Kj: 970/4628   Total fat: 47 g
Cals/Kj per portion: 242/1157   Fat per portion: 11.9 g

SEA BASS ROASTED WITH FENNEL

1.2 kg (2½ lb) sea bass without head, scaled and
   gutted
4 rosemary sprigs and 4 oregano sprigs
3 large fennel bulbs
salt and freshly ground black pepper
3 tablespoons olive oil
juice of 1 lemon
4 tablespoons chopped fresh oregano and parsley
150 ml (5 fl oz/⅔ cup) dry white wine
8 large green olives, stoned

Preheat oven to 220 C (425F/Gas 7). Wash
fish inside and out and pat dry on absorbent
kitchen paper. Lay it in an oval ovenproof
dish. Fill cavity with sprigs of rosemary.

Cut fennel bulbs in half lengthways, cut out
core and slice the bulbs thickly. Blanch in
boiling salted water for 5 minutes. Drain.
Whisk oil, lemon juice, chopped herbs, salt
and pepper together in a medium bowl. Stir
in the fennel, turning until coated. Spoon
the fennel over and around the fish, and
pour over any remaining marinade. Spoon
the wine over top and scatter with olives.

Bake in oven for 15 minutes, then spoon the
cooking juices over the fish and gently stir
the fennel around. Bake for a further 15
minutes. Turn off the oven and leave fish for
5 minutes before serving. Garnish with
oregano sprigs and serve with mixed rice.

Serves 4.

Total Cals/Kj: 1364/5710   Total fat: 58.9 g.
Cals/Kj per portion: 341/1428   Fat per portion: 14.7 g

SKEWERED TUNA ROLLS

700 g (1½ lb) fresh tuna, sliced 0.5 cm (¼ in) thick
1 tablespoon chopped fresh sage
1 tablespoon chopped fresh rosemary
2 dried bay leaves, crumbled
1 teaspoon dried chilli flakes
salt and freshly ground black pepper
fresh bay leaves
2 lemons, each cut into 6 wedges
1 tablespoon olive oil
1 tablespoon lemon juice

Soak 4 bamboo skewers in cold water for 30 minutes. Meanwhile, preheat grill. Place tuna slices between sheets of plastic wrap and beat gently with a rolling pin until thin.

Mix sage, rosemary, dried bay leaves and the spices together. Sprinkle mixture over tuna slices and season with salt and pepper. Roll up each slice of tuna neatly. Thread onto bamboo skewers, alternately with the fresh bay leaves and lemon wedges.

Brush with olive oil and lemon juice. Grill (or barbecue, if preferred) for 2-3 minutes on each side until just cooked. Serve with a green salad.

Serves 4.

Total Cals/Kj: 952/3983   Total fat: 32 g
Cals/Kj per portion: 283/995   Fat per portion: 8 g

Variation: Use swordfish instead of tuna. Ask the fishmonger to slice it thinly or buy it in a piece, then chill and slice it yourself.

SEAFOOD COUS-COUS

1.8 kg (4 lb) mixed whole, cleaned fish
450 g (1 lb) fresh mussels, cleaned
5 tablespoons olive oil
4 medium leeks, washed and sliced
2 medium bulbs florence fennel, sliced
4 cloves garlic, crushed
700 g (1½ lb) ripe red plum tomatoes, roughly
   chopped
0.4 g saffron threads
2 tablespoons sun-dried tomato paste or concentrate
1 teaspoon fennel seeds
115 ml (4 fl oz/½ cup) white wine
685 ml (24 fl oz/3 cups) fish stock
4 large raw shell-on prawns
500 g (1 lb 2 oz) cous-cous
salt and freshly ground pepper

Chop fish, including the bones, into large
chunks and place them in a large bowl in the
refrigerator. Place mussels in a bowl of cold
water. In a large pot, heat oil, add leeks and
fennel and cook gently for about 5 minutes
until softening, then add garlic, tomatoes,
saffron, tomato paste, fennel seeds, wine and
fish stock. Cover and boil for 20 minutes to
emulsify the oil. Add the fish and prawns,
bring to the boil again, then partly cover
and simmer for a further 20 minutes. Drain
the mussels and add them to the soup. Cover
and simmer for 5 minutes.

Strain soup through a fine sieve or colander
lined with muslin into another pan. Discard
solids. Season the soup. Cook the cous-cous
according to packet instructions. Reheat
soup. Place cous-cous in a warm terracotta
bowl. Pour over half the soup, cover and rest
for 30 minutes. Fork up grains and serve in
bowls with rest of soup served separately.

Serves 6.

Total Cals/Kj: 2039/8518   Total fat: 67 g
Cals/Kj per portion: 340/1420   Fat per portion: 11 g

—— RED MULLET PACKAGES ——

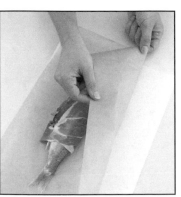

four 225 g (8 oz) red mullet, cleaned and scaled
2 tablespoons olive oil
4 fresh bay leaves
4 sage leaves
salt and pepper
4 thin slices prosciutto
sage sprigs, to garnish

Preheat oven to 190C (375F/Gas 5). Cut 4 rectangles of baking parchment big enough to wrap each red mullet generously. Brush the rectangles with the oil. Place a bay leaf in the cavity of each fish.

Lay a sage leaf on the side of each fish and season with salt and pepper. Wrap each fish in a slice of prosciutto.

Lay the fish on one half of the paper, fold over the other half loosely and twist the edges together to seal. Repeat with all the other fish. Lay them on a baking tray and bake in the oven for 25 minutes. Serve at once, opening the packages at the table. Garnish with sage and serve with broccoli and parsley cous-cous.

Serves 4.

Total Cals/Kj: 928/3870   Total fat: 39 g
Cals/Kj per portion: 232/967   Fat per portion: 9.9 g

───── TROTA IN BLU ─────

4 very fresh trout, gutted through gills, if possible,
  taking care not to remove the slime that covers the
  fish and will make it turn a bluish colour when
  cooked in the vinegar
3 tablespoons wine vinegar
lemon wedges and parsley sprigs, to garnish
FOR THE COURT BOUILLON:
1 onion, 1 carrot and 1 stick celery, sliced
2 sprigs each parsley and thyme
1 bay leaf
85 ml (3 fl oz/⅓ cup) white wine vinegar
salt and 4 peppercorns, crushed

Place trout in a dish and sprinkle with the
3 tablespoons vinegar. Cover and chill.

Meanwhile, to make the court bouillon, put
onion, carrot, celery, herbs and vinegar in a
large saucepan with a little salt, peppercorns
and 1.4 litres (50 fl oz/16¼ cups) water. Bring
to the boil, turn down heat, cover the pan
and simmer for 30 minutes. Strain and
return to the pan. Heat to barely simmering.

Uncover trout, drop them into the liquid,
two at a time, if pan is not large enough to
take all of them, and cook for 7-8 minutes.
They will turn a grey-blue and curl slightly.
Remove as soon as they are done. Arrange
on a platter and garnish with lemon wedges
and parsley sprigs. Serve with new potatoes
and green beans.

Serves 4.

Total Cals/Kj: 784/3280   Total fat: 26.6 g
Cals/Kj per portion: 196/820   Fat per portion: 6.6 g

─ROASTED GREY MULLET─

1.5 kg (3¼-3½ lb) grey mullet, cleaned
salt and freshly ground pepper
1 bay leaf
1 sprig rosemary
6 tablespoons olive oil
juice of two small lemons
1 teaspoon dried oregano
1 tablespoon chopped fresh parsley
2 cloves garlic, finely chopped
bay leaves and lemon wedges, to serve

Preheat grill. Season cavity of fish with salt and pepper. Place one bay leaf and rosemary inside the fish.

Grill (or barbecue) the mullet over medium heat for about 8 minutes on each side.

Whisk together oil, lemon juice, oregano, parsley and garlic until thick. Lay the fish on a serving platter and garnish with bay leaves and lemon wedges. Pour the sauce over the fish and serve at once, with new potatoes and leeks.

Serves 6.

Total Cals/Kj: 1734/7252   Total fat: 104 g
Cals/Kj per portion: 289/1209   Fat per portion: 17 g

—MONKFISH IN CITRUS SAUCE—

800 g (1¼ lb) trimmed monkfish, cut into chunks
2 tablespoons seasoned flour
2 tablespoons olive oil
finely grated rind and juice of 1 lemon and 1 orange
70 ml (2½ fl oz/⅓ cup) dry white wine
2 tablespoons chopped fresh parsley
salt and freshly ground black pepper

Toss monkfish in the seasoned flour and shake off the excess.

Heat oil in a non-stick frying pan, add fish and fry until golden all over. Add the citrus rinds and juices and wine, then cook over high heat to evaporate the alcohol. Turn down heat and simmer gently for 3 minutes.

Add chopped parsley and salt and pepper to taste. Lift the fish out and place on a serving dish. Reduce the sauce a little more and pour it over the fish. Serve at once, with new potatoes and sugar snap peas.

Serves 4.

Total Cals/Kj: 973/4071   Total fat: 36.5 g
Cals/Kj per portion: 243/1017   Fat per portion: 9 g

—MUSSELS ALLA MARINARA—

2 kg (2¼ lb) live mussels
1 tablespoon olive oil
4 cloves garlic, chopped
4 tablespoons chopped fresh parsley
½ teaspoon chilli flakes
115 ml (4 fl oz/½ cup) dry white wine
300 ml (10 fl oz/1¼ cups) passata
salt and freshly ground pepper
crusty bread, to serve

Scrub and de-beard mussels. Wash in several changes of water and discard any that are not firmly closed.

Put mussels in a large saucepan and place over high heat. Cover and shake pan over the heat until they all open. Transfer from the pan to a bowl. Strain the cooking juices into a jug.

Heat oil and fry garlic until golden. Add half the parsley, the chilli flakes, white wine, passata and mussel liquor. Bring to the boil, season well and add mussels. Heat through for 4 minutes, then scatter the remaining chopped parsley over the top. Serve at once, with crusty bread.

Serves 4.

Total Cals/Kj: 803/3359   Total fat: 26 g
Cals/Kj per portion: 201/840   Fat per portion: 6.5 g

—MIXED VEGETABLE FRITATTA—

225 g (8 oz) fresh asparagus
175 g (6 oz) small new potatoes
225 g (8 oz) frozen broad beans, thawed
4 eggs
2 egg whites
salt and freshly ground black pepper
3 tablespoons chopped mixed herbs
45 g (1½ oz) butter
25 g (1 oz) freshly grated Parmesan cheese

Trim asparagus. Steam for 12 minutes until tender, then plunge into cold water to set the colour and cool completely.

Meanwhile, cook potatoes in boiling salted water for 15-20 minutes until tender. Cool and thickly slice. Slip beans out of their skins. Drain and dry asparagus and cut into short lengths. Mix with beans. Beat eggs and egg whites together with good pinch of salt, and plenty of pepper. Stir in asparagus, beans and herbs. Melt the butter in a 25 cm (10 in) heavy non-stick frying pan. When foaming, pour in egg mixture. Turn down heat as low as possible and cook for about 15 minutes, until set and top is a little runny. Preheat grill.

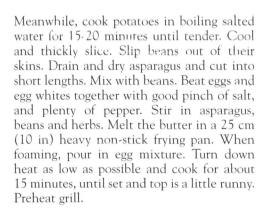

Scatter cooked sliced potato over the egg mixture and sprinkle with Parmesan cheese. Place under hot grill to lightly brown the cheese and just set the top. It should not brown too much or it will dry out. Serve immediately with salad.

Serves 4.

Total Cals/Kj: 1128/4695   Total fat: 75.6 g
Cals/Kj per portion: 282/1174   Fat per portion: 18.9 g

──VEGETABLES "A SCAPECE"──

350 g (12 oz) medium courgettes (zucchini)
350 g (12 oz) medium carrots
4 tablespoons olive oil
salt and freshly ground black pepper
2 tablespoons chopped fresh mint
2 tablespoons white wine vinegar
extra mint sprigs, to garnish

Trim and diagonally slice the courgettes (zucchini) and carrots, about 3 mm (⅛ in) thick.

Heat oil in a heavy non-stick frying pan and fry vegetables in batches until golden brown. Remove to a bowl with a slotted spoon as they are ready, leaving any oil in the bottom of the pan. Season vegetables to taste with salt and pepper.

Add mint and vinegar to the pan, bring to boil and immediately pour the mixture over the vegetables. Toss carefully to mix, then leave to stand at room temperature for at least 30 minutes to allow the flavours to develop. Garnish with extra mint and serve.

Serves 6.

Total Cals/Kj: 564/2323   Total fat: 47 g
Cals/Kj per portion: 94/387   Fat per portion: 7.8 g

GLAZED BABY ONIONS

575 g (1¼ lb) pickling onions
55 g (2 oz) unsalted butter
1 tablespoon caster sugar
salt and freshly ground black pepper
100 ml (3½ fl oz/ ⅓ cup) chicken or vegetable stock

Peel onions by plunging them into boiling water for 1 minute, then drain well and refresh under cold running water and peel off the skins.

Melt the butter in a heavy non-stick pan and add onions in a single layer. Sprinkle the sugar over them and add salt and pepper to taste. Cover and cook over very gentle heat for 20-30 minutes until the onions are tender and caramelized, shaking pan often.

Add the stock, bring to the boil and simmer without the lid for 5 minutes or until the sauce is syrupy. Serve immediately.

Serves 4.

Total Cals/Kj: 582/2427   Total fat: 46.5 g
Cals/Kj per portion: 145/607   Fat per portion: 11.6 g

GARLIC POTATOES

450 g (1 lb) medium-sized waxy potatoes
4 tablespoons olive oil
4 cloves garlic, unpeeled
few sprigs of thyme or rosemary
crystal rock salt, to sprinkle
extra herbs, to garnish

Cut potatoes lengthways into quarters and place in a bowl of cold water. Rinse under cold running water and pat completely dry with absorbent kitchen paper.

Heat oil in a flameproof casserole and when smoking hot, add the potatoes and garlic. Reduce heat and brown the potatoes on all sides. Stir in sprigs of herbs, cover and allow to cook in their own steam for 15 minutes.

Remove casserole lid and increase heat to evaporate any water and crisp the potatoes. Tip into a warm serving dish, if wished, and scatter with plenty of salt and more herbs.

Serves 4.

Total Cals/Kj: 711/2998   Total fat: 45 g
Cals/Kj per portion: 178/750   Fat per portion: 11.3 g

—BRAISED ARTICHOKES & PEAS—

2 tablespoons olive oil
6 spring onions, chopped
1 clove garlic, crushed
12 fresh baby artichokes
lemon juice
1 kg (2 lb) fresh peas, shelled, or 300 g (10 oz)
 frozen petits pois, thawed
2 tablespooons chopped fresh parsley
salt and freshly ground black pepper

Heat oil in a flameproof casserole, add the spring onions and garlic and cook gently for about 5 minutes until beginning to soften. Set aside.

Trim artichoke stalks to about 1 cm (½ in). Break off tough outside leaves, starting at the base, until you expose a central core of pale leaves. Slice off tough green or purple tips. With a small sharp knife, pare dark green skin from base and down stem. Cut artichokes in half and brush the cut parts with lemon juice to prevent browning.

Add artichokes and 85 ml (3 fl oz/½ cup) water to the onions. Cover and simmer for 10 minutes or until almost tender. Gently stir in the peas and a little extra water, if necessary. Cover and cook for 10 minutes, if using fresh peas, 5 minutes if frozen ones. Stir in parsley, season to taste with salt and pepper and serve at once.

Serves 6.

Total Cals/Kj: 540/2284   Total fat: 26 g
Cals/Kj per portion: 90/381   Fat per portion: 4.3 g

TOMATOES WITH GARLIC CRUST

6 slices stale bread
55 g (2 oz) anchovies in oil, drained
6 cloves garlic, finely chopped
3 tablespoons chopped fresh parsley
salt and freshly ground pepper
700 g (1½ lb) small plum tomatoes
3 tablespoons olive oil
extra chopped fresh parsley, to garnish

Preheat oven to 220C (425F/Gas 7). Tear up bread and place in a food processor with anchovies. Blend bread to crumbs, then dry-fry in a frying pan until crumbs are golden. Stir in garlic, parsley, salt and pepper.

Halve tomatoes around middle and place cut side up, close together in a single layer in a shallow roasting tin or dish. Sprinkle the breadcrumb mixture evenly over tomatoes and drizzle with olive oil.

Bake in oven for about 20 minutes until crust is golden and tomatoes are soft. The tomatoes will slightly disintegrate under the crust. Garnish with more chopped parsley and serve at once.

Serves 6.

Total Cals/Kj: 951/4026   Total fat: 38 g
Cals/Kj per portion: 158/671   Fat per portion: 6.3 g

──────RICE-FILLED TOMATOES──────

4 ripe beefsteak tomatoes
salt and freshly ground black pepper
150 g (5 oz) cooked rice
1 tablespoon pine nuts
1 tablespoon raisins, soaked in hot water
1 celery stick, finely chopped
2 tablespoons chopped fresh basil
2 teaspoons balsamic vinegar
2 tablespoons olive oil

Preheat oven to 170C (325F/Gas 3). Slice a lid off tomatoes; reserve. Scoop out flesh and sprinkle insides of tomatoes with salt. Invert and drain on kitchen paper for 15 minutes.

Sieve tomato pulp and mix into the cooked rice with pine nuts, raisins, celery and half the basil. Season well and use this to fill the tomatoes. Replace lids and place tomatoes in an oiled shallow ovenproof dish. Bake in oven for 45 minutes.

Whisk the vinegar with the oil. Remove the tomatoes from the oven, take off the lids and drizzle each one with the oil and vinegar. Replace the lids and leave to cool. Serve at room temperature, garnished with the rest of the basil.

Serves 4.

Total Cals/Kj: 619/2610   Total fat: 35.5 g
Cals/Kj per portion: 155/653   Fat per portion: 8.9 g

TOMATO & AUBERGINE GRATIN

1 medium aubergine (eggplant)
salt and freshly ground pepper
450 g (1 lb) ripe red tomatoes
150 ml (5 fl oz/⅔ cup) olive oil
3 tablespoons freshly grated Parmesan cheese

Using a sharp knife, slice the aubergine
(eggplant) into 3 mm (⅛ in) slices. Sprinkle
with salt and place in a colander to drain for
30 minutes. Rinse well and pat dry with
absorbent kitchen paper.

Preheat oven to 200C (400F/Gas 6). Halve
tomatoes through the middle. Heat oil in a
frying pan and fry the aubergine (eggplant)
slices in batches until golden brown. Drain
on absorbent kitchen paper.

Arrange the tomato halves and aubergine
(eggplant) slices haphazardly in a shallow
ovenproof dish. Season with salt and pepper
and sprinkle with Parmesan cheese. Bake in
the oven for 10-15 minutes until browned.
Cool slightly and serve warm.

Serves 6.

Total Cals/Kj: 1336/5599   Total fat: 127 g
Cals/Kj per portion: 223/933   Fat per portion: 21 g

FENNEL WITH LEMON & OLIVES

3 large fennel bulbs
grated rind and juice of 1 lemon
6 tablespoons olive oil
salt and freshly ground black pepper
12 black or green olives
2 tablespoons chopped fresh parsley

Preheat oven to 200C (400F/Gas 6). Trim
fennel and cut away any bruised parts. Cut
off fibrous tops, halve the bulbs lengthways
and cut out the core.

Place the bulbs cut side up in a baking dish.
Finely grate the rind from the lemon, then
squeeze the juice. Mix the lemon rind with
the juice and olive oil, salt and pepper.

Pour lemon mixture over the fennel, scatter
the olives over the top and bake in oven for
15 minutes. Turn fennel over and bake for a
further 15 minutes. Turn it once more and
bake for a final 15 minutes until very soft.
Sprinkle with the parsley and serve.

Serves 4.

Total Cals/Kj: 712/2975   Total fat: 71.3 g
Cals/Kj per portion: 178/744   Fat per portion: 17.8 g

TUSCAN BEAN & TOMATO STEW

450 g (1 lb) dried white haricot or cannellini beans,
soaked in cold water for several hours or overnight
350 g (12 oz) soft, ripe tomatoes or 400g can
chopped plum tomatoes, drained
4 tablespoons olive oil
3 cloves garlic, chopped
3 fresh sage leaves
salt and freshly ground black pepper
sage leaves, to garnish

Drain and rinse beans. Place in a saucepan
and cover with cold water. Bring to boil and
boil fiercely for 15 minutes. Drain.

Pass the tomatoes through a mouli-legumes
or purée in a blender, then pass the purée
through a sieve.

Heat oil in a large saucepan and add garlic
and sage. Cook over gentle heat until garlic
is golden brown. Stir in beans, then tomato
purée. Bring to boil, then reduce heat and
simmer gently for 20 minutes or until beans
are no longer crunchy but still firm. Taste
and season with salt and pepper. Garnish
with sage leaves and serve at once.

Serves 8.

Total Cals/Kj: 1743/7394   Total fat: 52 g
Cals/Kj per portion: 218/924   Fat per portion: 6.5 g

CAPONATA

4 medium aubergines (eggplants), cubed
salt and freshly ground pepper
5 tablespoons olive oil
1 medium onion, chopped
6 really ripe red tomatoes, skinned and chopped
6 celery sticks, chopped
1 tablespoon salted capers, rinsed well
55 g (2 oz) green olives
3 tablespoons red wine vinegar
1 tablespoon sugar
chopped fresh parsley, to garnish

Place aubergines (eggplants) in a colander, sprinkle with salt and leave to disgorge for 30 minutes. Rinse and pat dry.

Preheat oven to 200C (400F) Gas 6. Toss aubergines (eggplants) with oil in a roasting pan and roast for 20 minutes until golden brown, stirring occasionally. Remove with a slotted spoon and set aside. Pour the residual olive oil into a flameproof casserole or a saucepan and add onion. Cook for 5 minutes until soft. Add the tomatoes and cook for 15 minutes until tomatoes are pulpy.

Add all remaining ingredients, except aubergines (eggplants) and garnish, to sauce and simmer for 15 minutes. Season well and stir in the aubergines (eggplants). Allow to stand for at least 30 minutes to allow the flavours to develop before serving. Serve warm or cold, sprinkled with parsley.

Serves 6.

Total Cals/Kj: 819/3412   Total fat: 65 g
Cals/Kj per portion: 137/569   Fat per portion: 10.8 g

PEPERONATA

3 tablespoons olive oil
2 medium onions, sliced
3 cloves garlic, chopped
2 medium yellow peppers (capsicums)
2 medium red peppers (capsicums)
900 g (2 lb) fresh ripe tomatoes or two 400 g cans
  chopped tomatoes
salt and freshly ground black pepper

Heat olive oil in a saucepan or flameproof casserole, add onions and garlic and cook over very gentle heat for at least 20 minutes until golden and caramelized.

Halve and seed peppers (capsicums) and cut into thin strips. Add to onions and cook for 5 minutes until softened.

Skin, core, seed and chop tomatoes, then stir into pepper (capsicum) mixture. Simmer uncovered for 30-45 minutes until mixture is soft, thick and reduced. Taste and season with salt and pepper. Serve warm or cold.

Serves 4.

Total Cals/Kj: 761/3214   Total fat: 38.4 g
Cals/Kj per portion: 190/804   Fat per portion: 9.6 g

BASIC TOMATO SAUCE

1 kg (2 lb) fresh ripe tomatoes or the equivalent
  weight of drained, canned tomatoes
1 medium onion
2 garlic cloves
4 fresh basil leaves, bruised
3 tablespoons olive oil

Rinse fresh tomatoes, cut into quarters and
place in a large saucepan. Chop onion and
garlic and add to tomatoes. If using canned
tomatoes, roughly chop them and add the
onion and garlic as before. Cover, bring to
the boil, then cook slowly for 25 minutes.

Uncover saucepan and simmer for another
15-30 minutes to evaporate any extra liquid
– the sauce should be quite thick.

Pass the sauce through a mouli-legumes, or
purée in a blender, then sieve to remove any
seeds and skin. Stir in the basil and oil. The
sauce is ready to use and may be kept in a
covered container in the refrigerator for up
to 1 week. Serve hot or cold.

Serves 4.

Total Cals/Kj: 467/1950   Total fat: 35.9 g
Cals/Kj per portion: 117/487   Fat per portion: 9 g

DEVILLED STEAKS

1 tablespoon olive oil
4 fillet steaks, about 115 g (4 oz) each
salt and freshly ground pepper
2 tablespoons sherry vinegar
6 tablespoons dry red wine
4 tablespoons strong beef stock
2 cloves garlic, chopped
1 teaspoon crushed fennel seeds
1 tablespoon sun-dried tomato purée
large pinch chilli powder
chopped fresh parsley and parsley sprigs, to garnish

Heat oil in a non-stick frying pan until smoking, then add the steaks.

Cook for 2 minutes, turn over and cook for a further 2 minutes for medium/rare steaks. Cook for a little longer if well-done steaks are preferred. Remove from the pan, season and keep warm while making sauce. Pour vinegar, red wine and stock into the pan and boil for 30 seconds. Stir in garlic and fennel seeds. Whisk in the sun-dried tomato purée and chilli powder, to taste. Simmer until the sauce is syrupy.

Place steaks on warm plates. Pour any juices into the sauce, bring to the boil, taste and season. Pour sauce over the steaks. Garnish with chopped parsley and parsley sprigs and serve with grilled tomatoes and roasted diced potatoes.

Serves 4.

Total Cals/Kj: 752/3160   Total fat: 32 g
Cals/Kj per portion: 188/790   Fat per portion: 8 g

STEAK WITH TOMATO & OLIVES

four 115 g (4 oz) minute steaks
2 tablespoons olive oil
2 cloves garlic, chopped
1 medium onion, thinly sliced
1 carrot, finely diced
400 g can chopped tomatoes
1 teaspoon balsamic vinegar
½ teaspoon dried oregano
1 tablespoon chopped fresh basil
salt and freshly ground black pepper
12 Greek-style black olives, stoned
basil leaves, to garnish

Lightly brush both sides of the steaks with a little of the olive oil. Set aside.

In a non stick saucepan, heat remaining oil and add garlic. Cook gently until golden. Add onion and carrot and 2 tablespoons water. Cover saucepan and cook gently for 10 minutes until onions are soft, stirring once. Stir in the tomatoes, vinegar, herbs and seasoning, then simmer, uncovered, for 15 minutes until thick and reduced. Stir in the olives and keep warm.

Heat a ridged griddle until smoking and grill steaks for 1 minute per side. Remove to 4 warm plates and season with salt and pepper. Serve with the tomato and olive sauce (see Note). Garnish with basil leaves and serve with roasted sliced potatoes and broccoli.

Serves 4.

Total Cals/Kj: 944/3955　　　Total fat: 48 g
Cals/Kj per portion: 236/989　　Fat per portion: 12 g

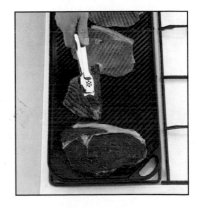

BEEF IN BAROLO WINE

1 kg (2¼ lb) braising beef joint
6 cloves garlic, crushed
1 onion, roughly chopped
1 carrot, chopped
1 stick of celery, chopped
2 bay leaves
2 large thyme sprigs
2-3 peppercorns, lightly crushed
2 cloves
2 allspice berries, crushed
115 ml (4 fl oz/½ cup) Barolo wine, or other
  full-bodied red wine
2 tablespoons tomato purée (paste)
150 ml (5 fl oz/⅔ cup) strong beef stock
salt and freshly ground black pepper

Place meat in a large polythene bag with the garlic, onion, carrot, celery, bay leaves, thyme, peppercorns, cloves, allspice and wine. Shake the bag, seal and refrigerate for several hours or overnight, turning meat occasionally. Next day, preheat oven to 170C (325F) Gas 3. Open bag, remove the meat from marinade and pat dry. Heat oil in a large flameproof casserole and brown the meat all over. Pour in reserved marinade, tomato purée (paste) and stock. Cover tightly and bake in oven for 2-3 hours until beef is tender.

Lift meat out of casserole and keep warm. Skim off any fat, remove bay leaves from the sauce. Purée in a blender or food processor until smooth. Taste and season. The sauce should be quite thick; if it is not, boil to reduce it. Slice the meat thinly and serve with the sauce, accompanied by mange-tout and polenta.

Serves 8.

Total Cals/Kj: 1424/5983   Total fat: 46.9 g
Cals/Kj per portion: 178/748   Fat per portion: 5.8 g

ITALIAN MEATBALLS

6 tablespoons semi-skimmed milk
1 slice bread, crusts removed
700 g (1½ lb) lean minced beef or lamb
6 spring onions, chopped
1 clove garlic, chopped
2 tablespoons freshly grated Parmesan cheese
freshly grated nutmeg
salt and freshly ground pepper
2 tablespoons olive oil
150 ml (5 fl oz/⅔ cup) dry white wine
400 g can chopped tomatoes

Sprinkle milk over the bread in a shallow dish and leave to soak for a few minutes.

Preheat oven to 180C (350F) Gas 4. Put meat in a large bowl and add soaked bread, spring onions, garlic, cheese, nutmeg and salt and pepper to taste. Work together until well mixed and smooth. With wet hands, roll into 30-36 even-sized balls. Heat the oil in a large non-stick frying pan and brown the meatballs in batches, then transfer them to a shallow ovenproof dish. Pour wine and tomatoes into frying pan and bring to boil, scraping up any sediment from the bottom of the pan.

Pour the sauce over the meatballs, cover and bake in oven for 1 hour until tender. Serve with buttered noodles.

Serves 8.

Total Cals/Kj: 2205/9236   Total fat: 147 g
Cals/Kj per portion: 275/1155   Fat per portion: 18.3 g

VEAL SCALOPPINE

four 115 g (4 oz) veal or turkey escalopes
2 tablespoons plain flour
salt and freshly ground pepper
3 tablespoons olive oil
3 tablespoons lemon juice
6 tablespoons white wine
2 tablespoons chopped fresh parsley
lemon wedges, to garnish

Trim escalopes of any gristle around edge.
Place the escalopes between sheets of plastic
film and bat out thinly without tearing. Coat
in the flour seasoned with salt and pepper.

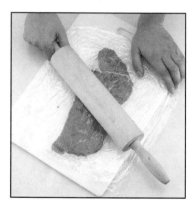

Heat the oil in a non-stick frying pan. Add
escalopes and fry over brisk heat for about
2 minutes per side, pressing them down with
a fish slice to keep them flat. Remove from
the pan and keep warm.

Add the lemon juice and wine to the frying
pan, stirring and scraping to dislodge any
sediment. Boil for 1 minute, then taste and
season. Stir in parsley and pour the lemon
sauce over escalopes. Garnish with lemon
wedges and serve at once, with potatoes and
stir-fried vegetables.

Serves 4.

Total Cals/Kj: 960/4023   Total fat: 45.8 g
Cals/Kj per portion: 240/1006   Fat per portion: 11.4 g

SALTIMBOCCA

eight 55 g (2 oz) veal or turkey escalopes
8 thin slices of Parma ham
salt and freshly ground pepper
8 fresh sage leaves
1 tablespoon olive oil
25 g (1 oz) butter
70 ml (2½ fl oz/⅓ cup) dry Marsala or sherry
fresh sage leaves, to garnish

Trim escalopes of any gristle around edge.
Place between sheets of plastic film and bat
out thinly without tearing. Trim Parma ham
of any fat and cut to same size as escalopes.

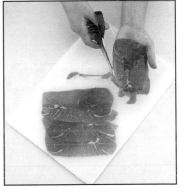

Season each escalope with a little salt. Place
a sage leaf on top of each one and cover with
a slice of ham. Secure each one through the
middle with a wooden cocktail stick, as if
taking a large stitch. These are not rolled up.

Heat the oil and butter in a non-stick frying
pan and fry the escalopes in batches, on
both sides for about 2 minutes until golden
and tender. Remove and keep warm. Add
the Marsala to the pan, stir and bring to the
boil, then boil for 1 minute. Spoon the sauce
over escalopes, garnish with sage and serve
with green beans and noodles.

Serves 4.

Total Cals/Kj: 944/3935   Total fat: 54 g
Cals/Kj per portion: 236/984   Fat per portion: 13.6 g

──SKEWERED MEAT ROLLS──

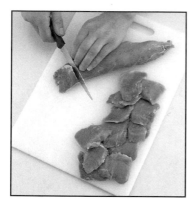

800 g (1¼ lb) fillet of lamb, beef or pork
225 g (8 oz) low-fat mozzarella cheese
salt and freshly ground pepper
fresh basil or sage leaves
2 corn-on-the cob
1 aubergine (eggplant), cut into large cubes
3 medium courgettes (zucchini), cut into 2.5 cm
   (1 in) lengths
olive oil for basting

Soak 6 or 12 bamboo skewers in cold water. Cut the meat into thin slices, then place between sheets of plastic film and bat out thinly without tearing. Slice cheese thinly.

Season meat with salt and pepper and lay a piece of cheese on top of each escalope with a sage or basil leaf. Roll up each escalope like a sausage. Place in a dish, cover and chill in the refrigerator.

Meanwhile, cook the corn-on-the-cob in boiling salted water for 10 minutes, drain and refresh in cold water. Preheat grill. Slice corn cobs into 2.5 cm (1 in) thick rounds. Thread meat rolls and vegetables onto the skewers. Brush lightly with olive oil, place under the hot grill and grill for 3-4 minutes per side. Serve with rice and salad leaves.

Serves 6.

Total Cals/Kj: 2232/9347   Total fat: 122.8 g
Cals/Kj per portion: 372/1558   Fat per portion: 20.5 g

ROAST LEG OF LAMB WITH WINE

1 kg (2¼ lb) lean leg of lamb
2 tablespoons olive oil
55 g (2 oz) salted anchovies, boned and rinsed
2 cloves garlic, chopped
8 juniper berries
1 tablespoon chopped fresh rosemary
2 tablespoons balsamic vinegar
salt and freshly ground pepper
150 ml (5 fl oz/⅔ cup) dry white wine

Trim lamb of any excess fat. Heat oil in a flameproof casserole in which the lamb will fit snugly. Add the lamb and brown all over. Remove and leave to cool.

In a mortar, pound the anchovies, garlic, rosemary and 4 of the juniper berries to a paste. Stir in vinegar. Make small incisions all over the lamb with a small sharp knife. Spread paste all over lamb, working it into the slits. Season. Replace lamb in casserole, and pour in wine. Crush remaining juniper berries and add to the casserole. Cover and simmer for 1½-2 hours, until very tender, turning lamb every 20 minutes.

Carefully remove lamb from casserole and keep warm. Skim fat from sauce. Add a little water, if necessary, and bring to the boil, scraping the bottom of the pan to mix in the sediment. Serve the sauce with the lamb, accompanied by roast potatoes, carrots and mange-tout.

Serves 8.

Total Cals/Kj: 2085/8716   Total fat: 120 g
Cals/Kj per portion: 260/1089   Fat per portion: 15 g

—FLORENTINE ROAST PORK—

1 kg (2¼ lb) pork loin, boned
2 tablespoons chopped fresh rosemary leaves
2 cloves garlic, chopped
salt and freshly ground black pepper
3 tablespoons olive oil
150 ml (5 fl oz/⅔ cup) dry white wine

Preheat oven to 160C (325F) Gas 3. Using a flat skewer, make deep incisions all over the meat. Mix rosemary and garlic together with plenty of salt and pepper. Push the rosemary mixture into the incisions. Rub any remaining mixture into flap where the bones have been removed

Season very well and tie up neatly with string. Rub meat all over with olive oil and place in a roasting tin. Pour in white wine and roast in oven for 1½ hours, basting frequently and turning the joint each time. If you have a spit or rotisserie, roast it on the spit, basting frequently.

Transfer pork to a serving dish and keep warm. Skim fat off pan, and add a little water to the juices. Scrape up sediment and bring to boil, taste and season. Carve the pork into thick slices, garnish with rosemary sprigs and serve with the sauce, carrots and brown lentils.

Serves 6.

Total Cals/Kj: 1880/7859   Total fat: 104 g
Cals/Kj per portion: 313/1310   Fat per portion: 17.3 g

VENETIAN-STYLE LIVER

3 tablespoons olive oil
55 g (2 oz) butter
2 large onions, sliced
salt and freshly ground black pepper
12 slices calves' liver
1 teaspooon balsamic vinegar
2 teaspoons white wine vinegar
4 fresh sage leaves, shredded
lemon wedges, to garnish

Heat the oil and butter in a heavy non-stick frying pan and add onions. Cook very gently for about 20 minutes, until onions are very soft and beginning to brown slightly, stirring them occasionally.

Season well, remove with a slotted spoon and keep warm. Raise the heat, add liver to pan and fry on both sides for 2-3 minutes until browned (brown the liver in batches, if necessary).

If browning in batches, return all the liver to the pan. Add the vinegars, sage, salt and pepper to the pan, then add the onions. Toss together to heat through. Garnish with the lemon wedges and serve with courgettes (zucchini) and red lentils.

Serves 6.

Total Cals/Kj: 1764/7350 Total fat: 122.5 g
Cals/Kj per portion: 294/1225 Fat per portion: 20.4 g

CHICKEN & WILD MUSHROOMS

4 tablespoons olive oil
2 cloves garlic, crushed
4 boneless corn-fed chicken breasts
150 ml (5 fl oz/⅔ cup) dry white vermouth
salt and pepper
450 g (1 lb) mixed wild mushrooms or a mixture of
   cultivated mushrooms, such as brown cap, shiitake
   and oyster
2 tablespoons chopped fresh oregano
oregano sprigs, to garnish

Heat half the olive oil in a sauté pan. Add garlic and cook for 2 minutes until golden. Add chicken breasts, skin-side down and brown well on all sides.

Pour in the vermouth and season well with salt and pepper. Bring to the boil, cover and simmer for 20-30 minutes until tender.

Meanwhile, halve or slice the mushrooms, if large. Heat remaining oil, add mushrooms and sauté for 3-5 minutes until brown and tender, but still firm. Gently stir mushrooms and any cooking juices into the chicken with the chopped oregano. Garnish with oregano sprigs and serve at once with rice.

Serves 4.

Total Cals/Kj: 1442/6031   Total fat: 79.9 g
Cals/Kj per portion: 360/1508   Fat per portion: 19.9 g

——LEMON & CHILLI CHICKEN——

1.5 kg (3¼-3½ lb) corn-fed or free-range chicken,
  jointed into 8
4 ripe juicy lemons
8 cloves garlic
1 small red chilli, split, seeds removed, and chopped
1 tablespoon honey
4 tablespoons chopped fresh parsley
salt and freshly ground black pepper

Place chicken joints in a shallow ovenproof
baking dish. Squeeze juice from the lemons
and pour into a small bowl. Reserve the
lemon halves.

Remove skin from 2 of the garlic cloves,
crush them and add to lemon juice with the
chilli and honey. Stir well and pour mixture
over the chicken, tucking the lemon halves
around joints. Cover and leave to marinate
for at least 2 hours, turning once or twice.

Preheat oven to 200C (400F) Gas 6. Turn
the chicken skin side up and place lemon
halves cut side down around the joints with
the remaining whole garlic. Roast in oven
for 45 minutes or until golden brown and
tender. Stir in the parsley, taste and season.
Garnish with the roasted lemon halves and
serve with puréed potatoes.

Serves 4.

Total Cals/Kj: 1027/4299   Total fat: 38.5 g
Cals/Kj per portion: 257/1075   Fat per portion: 9.6 g

──CHICKEN UNDER A BRICK──

1.8 kg (4 lb) roasting chicken, preferably free-range
4 tablespoons olive oil
salt and freshly ground black pepper
chopped fresh parsley and lemon wedges, to serve

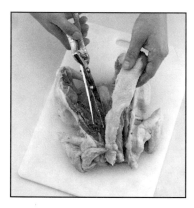

Using kitchen scissors or poultry shears, cut along either side of chicken's backbone and remove. Place chicken skin-side down, open out and press down hard to flatten. Turn skin-side up.

Make a slit through the skin at each side between breast and thigh. Fold the legs in and push the drumstick bone through each slit. The bird should be completely flat. Heat the oil in a large heavy frying pan and place chicken skin-side down in pan. Place a flat lid on top of the chicken and a 4.5 kg (10 lb) weight (bricks or stones) on top. Cook for 12 minutes over medium heat until golden.

Remove lid and weights, turn chicken over, season well and replace lid and weights. Cook for another 12-15 minutes or until tender and the juices run clear. Leave to rest in a warm place for 15-20 minutes before carving. Serve with chopped fresh parsley and lemon wedges, accompanied by new potatoes, carrots and courgettes (zucchini).

Serves 6.

Total Cals/Kj: 1554/6499   Total fat: 87 g
Cals/Kj per portion: 259/1083   Fat per portion: 14.5 g

CHICKEN CACCIATORA

4 rashers smoked streaky bacon, chopped
4 skinless chicken portions (about 800 g/1¾ lb)
2 cloves garlic, chopped
1 tablespoon balsamic vinagar
400 g can chopped tomatoes
150 ml (5 fl oz/⅔ cup) passata
150 ml (5 fl oz/⅔ cup) chicken stock
2 medium onions, roughly chopped
sprig of rosemary
1 bay leaf
salt and freshly ground black pepper
225 g (8 oz) mushrooms, thickly sliced
chopped fresh parsley, to garnish

Heat a non-stick frying pan, add bacon and fry until golden. Remove to a deep saucepan or flameproof casserole with a slotted spoon. In the fat remaining in the pan, fry the chicken pieces until well browned, then add to the bacon. Add garlic to frying pan and cook until golden. Deglaze the pan with the vinegar, scraping any sediment from base of pan. Pour in tomatoes, passata and stock and bring to boil. Stir in the onions, rosemary and bay leaf and season to taste.

Pour mixture over chicken and bring to the boil. Turn down heat, cover and simmer for 30 minutes. Stir in mushrooms, cover and simmer for 15 minutes. Uncover and simmer for a final 15 minutes to allow the sauce to evaporate and thicken. Garnish with plenty of chopped parsley and serve with ribbon pasta.

Serves 4.

Total Cals/Kj: 1320/5534   Total fat: 44 g
Cals/Kj per portion: 330/1384   Fat per portion: 11 g

—CHICKEN WITH SALSA VERDE—

4 small skinless chicken breasts
8 tablespoons chopped fresh parsley
1 clove garlic, finely chopped
4 tablespoons chopped fresh mint
1 tablespoon finely chopped capers
1 tablespoon finely chopped gherkins
finely grated rind and juice of 1 lemon
100 ml (3½ fl oz/⅓ cup) olive oil
salt and freshly ground black pepper

Place chicken breasts in a sauté pan, cover with water and bring to the boil. Simmer very gently for 15-20 minutes until cooked. Allow to cool completely in the water.

In a bowl, mix together the parsley, garlic, mint, capers, gherkins, lemon juice and rind. Gradually beat in olive oil and season to taste. Do not do this in a food processor or the texture will be ruined.

Thickly slice each chicken breast crossways and arrange on a plate, spoon a little salsa verde over it and serve the rest separately. Serve with salad.

Serves 4.

Total Cals/Kj: 1262/5279   Total fat: 94.5 g
Cals/Kj per portion: 316/1320   Fat per portion: 23.6 g

—PIGEON WITH CRISP POLENTA—

2 tablespoons chopped fresh sage
1 tablespoon chopped fresh rosemary
salt and freshly ground black pepper
115 g (4 oz/scant 1 cup) quick-cook polenta
1 tablespoon olive oil
8 pigeon breasts
pinch of ground allspice
1 quantity Basic Tomato Sauce (see page 65)
rosemary and sage sprigs, to garnish

Bring 550 ml (20 fl oz/2½ cups) water to the boil with chopped herbs, salt and pepper. Sprinkle in the polenta, whisking to prevent lumps forming.

Turn down heat and simmer the polenta for 5-10 minutes, stirring constantly until very thick. Turn out onto a wooden board and shape into a loaf with a spatula. Cool, cover and chill for 1 hour. Preheat the grill. Cut the polenta into 4 thick slices. Brush with some of the olive oil and grill on each side until crisp and golden. Keep warm.

Rub pigeon breasts with the allspice, then brush with a little olive oil. Place skin-side up on grill pan and grill for 4 minutes. Turn over and grill for another 2 minutes. Top each polenta slice with 2 pigeon breasts. Garnish with rosemary and sage sprigs and serve with the fresh tomato sauce.

Serves 4.

Total Cals/Kj: 1454/6079   Total fat: 65 g
Cals/Kj per portion: 364/1520   Fat per portion: 16 g

—RABBIT & RED PEPPER STEW—

1 kg (2¼ lb) rabbit pieces
2 tablespoons chopped fresh thyme
2 tablespoons chopped fresh rosemary
2 fresh bay leaves
juice of 1 lemon
1 tablespoon balsamic vinegar
salt and freshly ground black pepper
2 tablespoons olive oil
4 red peppers (capsicums), seeded and roughly diced
400 g can strained crushed tomatoes

Place rabbit in a plastic bag with the herbs, lemon juice, vinegar, salt and pepper. Seal and leave to marinate in the refrigerator for 2-3 hours or overnight.

Heat half the oil in a saucepan and add the peppers (capsicums) and cook over gentle heat for about 10 minutes until soft. Stir in tomatoes and season with salt and pepper. Cover and cook for 30 minutes. Remove the rabbit from marinade, reserving marinade, and pat dry.

Heat remaining oil in a frying pan, add the rabbit pieces and fry on all sides until golden. Add the rabbit to pepper (capsicum) sauce. Deglaze the frying pan with the reserved marinade and add to the rabbit. Cover and simmer for 20-30 minutes until the rabbit is tender. Serve with pasta.

Serves 4.

Total Cals/Kj: 1290/5399   Total fat: 52 g
Cals/Kj per portion: 322/1350   Fat per portion: 13 g

WATERMELON GRANITA

300 g (10 oz) caster sugar
2 cinnamon sticks
800 g (1¼ lb) skinned watermelon flesh
juice of 1 lemon
mint sprigs, to decorate

Put sugar and cinnamon sticks into a pan with 300 ml (10 fl oz/1¼ cups) water. Stir over gentle heat until sugar has dissolved, bring to boil and boil for 1 minute. Allow to cool completely, then remove, wash and dry the cinnamon sticks.

Pass the watermelon flesh through a mouli-legumes or mash, then sieve to remove the seeds. Mix watermelon pulp with the cold syrup, adding lemon juice to taste, then chill in refrigerator. Pour into a shallow container to a depth of 2 cm (¾ in). Cover and freeze for 1 hour until the liquid has formed an ice rim around the edge and is starting to freeze on the base.

Scrape this away with a fork and mash evenly with remaining liquid. Repeat every 30 minutes until mixture forms a smooth consistency of ice crystals. Serve mounded high in chilled glasses (frosted in freezer, if suitable), decorated with mint.

Serves 6.

Total Cals/Kj: 1430/6008   Total fat: 2.4 g
Cals/Kj per portion: 238/1001   Fat per portion: 0.4 g

COFFEE GRANITA

45 g (1½ oz) finely ground espresso coffee
finely grated rind of 1 lemon
150 g (5 oz/⅔ cup) caster sugar
1 tablespoon lemon juice

Put espresso coffee into a pan with 500 ml (18 fl oz/2¼ cups) water. Bring to the boil and remove from the heat. Add the lemon rind and leave to infuse for 5 minutes. Strain through a coffee filter.

Mix 150 ml (5 fl oz/⅔ cup) water with the caster sugar until dissolved. Stir in infused coffee and lemon juice, leave to cool, then chill in the refrigerator. Pour into a shallow container to a depth of 2 cm (¾ in). Cover and freeze for 1 hour until the liquid has formed an ice rim around the edge and is starting to freeze on the base.

Scrape away ice rim with a fork and mash evenly with the remaining liquid. Repeat every 30 minutes until the mixture forms a smooth consistency of ice crystals. Serve in chilled glasses (frosted in freezer, if suitable) with a dollop of whipped whipping cream, if wished.

Serves 8.

Total Cals/Kj: 591/2472   Total fat: 0 g
Cals/Kj per portion: 74/247   Fat per portion: 0 g

BISCOTTI & VIN SANTO

175 g (6 oz) whole blanched almonds, toasted
115 g (4 oz) unsalted butter, softened
200 g (7 oz) granulated sugar
2 eggs, beaten
finely grated rind of 1 orange
1½ teaspoons baking powder
½ teaspoon salt
85 g (3 oz) polenta
about 350 g (12 oz) plain white flour
Vin Santo, to serve

Coarsely chop one third of the almonds and mix these with the whole almonds. Cream butter with the sugar until just mixed. Beat in eggs, orange rind, baking powder and salt.

Stir in polenta, almonds and 300 g (10 oz) of the flour. Turn onto a floured work surface and knead to a smooth dough, adding the remaining flour little by little, until the dough is soft not sticky. Divide dough into 4 equal pieces and roll each into a sausage 5 cm (2 in) wide and 2 cm (¾ in) deep. Place them on 2 greased baking sheets and bake for about 35 minutes until just golden around the edges. Cool for 5 minutes.

Cut rolls diagonally into 1 cm (½ in) thick slices. Place the slices cut side down on the baking sheets and bake them for another 10 minutes until golden brown. Transfer to a wire rack to cool completely. Serve with small glasses of Vin Santo for dipping.

Makes about 50.

Total Cals/Kj: 4392/18347   Total fat: 212 6
Cals/Kj per biscuit: 88/367   Fat per biscuit: 4.2 g
Cals/Kj per glass Vin Santo: 70/293

—RICOTTA & COFFEE DESSERT—

350 g (12 oz) reduced-fat ricotta cheese, at room
   temperature
350 g (12 oz) reduced-fat cream cheese, at room
   temperature
1 tablespoon rum
2 tablespoons brandy or Tia Maria
few drops of vanilla essence
2 tablespoons espresso ground Italian roast coffee
3 tablespoons icing sugar
150 ml (5 fl oz/⅔ cup) whipping cream
55 g (2 oz) chocolate shavings, to decorate

Sieve ricotta and mascarpone together, then
beat with a wooden spoon. Do not attempt
to do this in a food processor.

Beat in the rum, brandy, vanilla and ground
coffee. Taste and add icing sugar. Carefully
spoon mixture into small freezerproof dishes
or demi-tasse cups, piling the mixture high.
Place in freezer for 30 minutes and transfer
to the refrigerator to soften slightly for about
10 minutes before serving it. The dessert
should be only just frozen or very chilled.

Just before serving, whisk the whipping
cream to soft peaks and spoon a blob on top
of each dessert, then sprinkle with chocolate
flakes. Place on saucers and serve at once.

Serves 6.

Total Cals/Kj: 1868/7704   Total fat: 119 g
Cals/Kj per portion: 311/1297   Fat per portion: 19.8 g

──────STRAWBERRY SORBET──────

250 g (9 oz/1¼ cups) caster sugar
450 g (1 lb) fresh sweet strawberries
1 tablespoon balsamic vinegar

Pour 250 ml (9 fl oz/1 cup) water into a
saucepan and add the sugar. Heat gently to
dissolve sugar, then bring to boil and boil for
1 minute. Cool then chill in refrigerator.
Meanwhile, wash and hull the strawberries.
Purée in a blender or food processor until
smooth, and pass through a sieve, if liked.
Chill the purée.

Stir the syrup into the chilled stawberry
purée and add the balsamic vinegar. Freeze
in an ice cream maker for the best results.

Alternatively, pour mixture into a shallow
freezer tray and freeze until the sorbet is
frozen around the edges. Mash well with a
fork, beat and refreeze until almost solid.
Repeat this twice more. Serve in chilled
glass dishes.

Serves 6.

Total Cals/Kj: 1118/4677   Total fat: 0 g
Cals/Kj per portion: 186/780   Fat per portion: 0 g

ORANGE SORBET

10 juicy oranges
200 g (7 oz/1 cup) caster sugar
2 tablespoons orange flower water

Pare the rind from the oranges with a potato peeler avoiding any white pith. Chop roughly. Squeeze the juice from the oranges and strain through a sieve.

Pour 200 ml (7 fl oz/¾ cup) water into a saucepan, add the sugar and heat gently to dissolve. Stir in the pared orange rind, juice, and the orange flower water. Boil rapidly for 1 minute. Cool, then chill in refrigerator. Strain the syrup.

Freeze in an ice cream maker for the best results. Alternatively, pour into a shallow freezer tray and freeze until the sorbet is frozen around the edges. Mash well with a fork, beat and refreeze until almost solid. Repeat this twice more. Serve in chilled glass dishes.

Serves 4.

Total Cals/Kj: 981/4115   Total fat: 0 g
Cals/Kj per portion: 245/1029   Fat per portion: 0 g

—LIGHT VANILLA ICE CREAM—

1 vanilla pod
1.1 litres (2 pints/5 cups) UHT lactose-reduced
  milk or semi-skimmed milk
4 tablespoons cornflour
275 g (9½ oz/1½ cups) caster sugar
few drops of vanilla essence

Split the vanilla pod in two and place in a saucepan with 900 ml (1½ pints/4 cups) milk. Heat to boiling point, remove from heat and leave to infuse for 20 minutes. Remove vanilla pod, scrape out seeds and whisk the seeds back into the milk. Wash and dry the pod and store in your sugar jar.

Dissolve the cornflour in the remaining milk and stir in the sugar. Pour this into the hot milk. Set over the heat again and bring to the boil, stirring constantly until thickened.

Cover the surface with plastic film and allow to cool to room temperature. Stir in the vanilla, chill, then freeze in an ice cream maker for best results. Alternatively, pour into a shallow freezer tray and freeze until ice cream is frozen around the edges. Mash well with a fork, beat and refreeze until almost solid. Repeat this twice more.

Serves 6.

Total Cals/Kj: 1802/7582   Total fat: 18 g
Cals/Kj per portion: 300/1264   Fat per portion: 3 g

──PEARS POACHED IN WINE──

1 vanilla pod
300 ml (10 fl oz/ 1¼ cups) sweet white wine
300 ml (10 fl oz/ 1¼ cups) Vin Santo
6 firm but ripe dessert pears
2 teaspoons arrowroot
few drops of vanilla essence
mint leaves, to decorate

Split vanilla pod and place in a saucepan with the wines and bring to the boil. Peel the pears carefully, but leave their stalks on.

Stand the pears in the pan – they should just fit. Spoon a little of the liquid over them to prevent discoloration. Cover tightly and simmer for about 25 minutes, turning in the liquid, until tender. Allow pears to cool in the liquid. Remove vanilla pod and scrape out the seeds and reserve them. Lift out the pears and place in a serving dish.

Add vanilla seeds to poaching liquid. Boil until liquid is reduced to 300 ml (10 fl oz/1¼ cups). Moisten arrowroot with a little water and mix into sauce. Boil until thickened. Stir in vanilla. Cool, then pour over pears.

Serves 6.

Total Cals/Kj: 996/4184   Total fat: 1.2 g
Cals/Kj per portion: 166/697   Fat per portion: 0 g

Note: Decorate with chopped nuts and mint if you like, but this will add extra calories.

CARAMEL ORANGES

4 large oranges, scrubbed
115 g (4 oz/½ cup) caster sugar
300 ml (10 fl oz/1¼ cups) orange juice
1 tablespoon orange liqueur

Remove the rind from the oranges, then remove pith as you would an apple, being careful not to leave any of the white pith behind. Cut the rind into fine needleshreds.

Slice each orange horizontally into rounds and re-form into oranges with the help of a cocktail stick. Place in a serving dish. Put the sugar into a heavy-based pan and add 55 ml (2 fl oz/¼ cup) of the orange juice. Heat gently to allow the sugar to melt and dissolve slowly, then boil until it turns a rich golden brown. Remove from heat and add the remaining orange juice, taking care as it will splutter.

Set on the heat again, add the needleshreds and stir until caramel has dissolved. Bring to the boil and boil until reduced and syrupy. Cool, then stir in the liqueur. Pour mixture over the oranges and serve.

Serves 4.

Total Cals/Kj: 816/3440   Total fat: 0.9 g
Cals/Kj per portion: 204/860   Fat per portion: 0 g

—FEATHER-LIGHT TIRAMISU—

3 tablespoons very strong cold espresso coffee
few drops of vanilla essence
1 tablespoon brandy or rum
100 g (3½ oz/⅓ cup) vanilla sugar (see page 94)
2 egg whites
225 g (8 oz) reduced-fat cream cheese
115 ml (4 fl oz/½ cup) reduced-fat crème fraîche
18 sponge fingers
55 g (2 oz) bitter (dark) chocolate, grated

In a bowl, mix together coffee, vanilla and brandy. In another bowl, beat sugar and cream cheese together. Whisk crème fraîche until just holding its shape and fold into the cream cheese mixture.

In a clean bowl, whisk the egg whites until forming soft peaks, then fold into the cheese and cream mixture.

Break half the sponge fingers into pieces and place on the bottom of 6 glasses. Drizzle with half the coffee mixture. Spoon on half the cream mixture and sprinkle with half the grated chocolate. Repeat with remaining ingredients, finishing with grated chocolate. Chill until firm and serve within 1 day.

Serves 6.

Total Cals/Kj: 1689/6298   Total fat: 73.8 g
Cals/Kj per portion: 282/1050   Fat per portion: 12 g

—BAKED RICOTTA CHEESECAKE—

350 g (12 oz) reduced-fat ricotta cheese
3 eggs, separated
100 g (3½ oz) caster sugar
3 tablespoons dark rum
1 teaspoon vanilla essence
finely grated rind of 2 lemons
55 g (2 oz) ground almonds
55 g (2 oz) sultanas, soaked in warm water and
  drained
fresh seasonal fruit, to serve

Preheat oven to 180C (350F) Gas 4. Grease,
lightly flour and base-line a 20 cm (8 in)
spring-form tin. Sieve the ricotta into a large
bowl and beat in the egg yolks and sugar.

Beat in rum, vanilla and lemon rind. Fold in
ground almonds and sultanas. Whisk the egg
whites until soft peaks form, then gently fold
them into the cheese mixture. Gently spoon
into prepared tin and level the surface. Bake
in oven for 30-40 minutes until firm and
slightly shrunken from the sides of the tin.

Open the oven door, swith off heat and
leave cheesecake inside to cool completely,
then chill in refrigerator. To serve, remove
cheesecake from tin and top with seasonal
fruit. Dust with icing sugar.

Serves 6.

Total Cals/Kj: 1679/6994   Total fat: 89 g
Cals/Kj per portion: 280/1166   Fat per portion: 14.8 g

ZABAGLIONE

4 egg yolks
70 g (2½ oz) vanilla sugar
115 ml (4 fl oz/½ cup) Marsala
sponge fingers, to serve

With an electric whisk, whisk the egg yolks
and sugar together in a large heatproof bowl
until pale and fluffy. Place bowl over a pan of
gently simmering water. Mix in the Marsala.

Start whisking slowly. Gradually whisk faster
until the mixture doubles in volume and
becomes very thick and glossy. Take care not
to overheat or the mixture will scramble.

Spoon the zabaglione into heatproof glasses
or ramekins and serve immediately with
sponge fingers.

Serves 6.

Total Cals/Kj: 683/2844   Total fat: 22.5 g
Cals/Kj per portion: 114/474   Fat per portion: 3.7 g

Note: To make vanilla sugar, simply store a
vanilla pod in a jar of sugar and leave for at
least 2-3 weeks for it to flavour the sugar.

WALNUT CAKE

350 g (12 oz) walnut pieces
4 eggs, sparated
225 g (8 oz/1¼ cups) caster sugar
finely grated rind of 1 lemon
icing sugar, to decorate

Preheat oven to 180C (350F) Gas 4. Grease, flour and base-line a 22.5 cm (9 in) spring-form tin. Grind the walnuts in a blender or food processor until fine but not greasy.

With an electric beater, whisk the egg yolks and sugar together until pale and creamy. Fold in the lemon rind and nuts. Whisk egg whites until stiff and carefully fold into the nut mixture. Gently pour into prepared tin.

Bake in oven for 45-60 minutes until risen and firm. Cool in the tin. It will shrink away from the edges. Remove from the tin and dredge with icing sugar. Serve in thin wedges with low-fat vanilla custard, if liked.

Serves 12.

Total Cals/Kj: 3653/15131   Total fat: 265.8 g
Cals/Kj per portion: 304/1261   Fat per portion: 22 g

INDEX